Money Counts

How Dollars Dominate
Illinois Politics and
What We Can Do About It

Kent D. Redfield, Ph.D.
University of Illinois at Springfield

THE INSTITUTE FOR PUBLIC AFFAIRS

University of Illinois at Springfield
Springfield, Illinois

Library of Congress Cataloging-in-Publication Data

Redfield, Kent.
   Money counts : how dollars dominate Illinois politics and what we can do about it /
Kent D. Redfield.
      p. cm.
   ISBN 0-938943-19-7 (alk. paper)
   1. Campaign funds--Illinois. I. Title.

JK1991.5.I3 R44 2000
324.7'8'09773--dc21
                                                                    00-056730

Copyright © 2001 by the University of Illinois at Springfield, Springfield, Illinois.

Production of this book was made possible by a grant from The Joyce Foundation.

Developmental Editor: Rodd Whelpley
Copyeditors: Beverley Scobell and Janelle Bandy
Cover and Text Designer: Diana L.C. Nelson
Printer: United Graphics

Printed in the United States of America

4 3 2 1   2001 2002 2003 2004

The Institute for Public Affairs
Institute Publications
P.O. Box 19243
University of Illinois at Springfield
Springfield, IL 62794-9243

Phone: 217-206-6502
Fax: 217-206-7257

E-mail: wojcicki@uis.edu

Web site: http://ipapublications.uis.edu

Contents

Preface

It's impossible to observe and study the often corrupting role of money in Illinois politics without forming strong opinions about right and wrong, and what should be done, and what can be done. There are fundamental problems in the Illinois political system that relate directly to money. *Money Counts* is my best assessment of the role cash plays in Illinois politics, the impact that it has on elections and public policy, and the immediate and midterm steps that would lessen the harmful effects that the completely unrestrained flow of money has on the current content and character of Illinois politics.

The Illinois political system is awash with money. For each election, campaign costs go up and up, and they are fueled, year after year, by the same well-heeled special-interest groups. The party leaders — that is, the president of the Senate and the speaker of the House and their minority counterparts — receive the lion's share of the campaign cash and dole it out to a few legislators involved in key races. The rest of the campaigns for the seats in the Illinois House and Senate are — by design — uncompetitive. Candidates for statewide offices grab a bundle every four years. Interest groups contribute to the nominees from both parties and even to incumbents running unopposed.

But the money doesn't stop after voting day. It keeps coming — especially when interest groups have business before the state's General Assembly. What do all those campaign contributions buy for the contributors? What is the correlation between those who make big campaign contributions and protectionist legislation, favorable tax laws, or "harmful" bills that get quashed in committee? When it comes to representing the citizens of Illinois, what is the cost of the cost of Illinois elections? When it comes to making public policy in Illinois, what is the cost of the wide openness of our campaign finance system? How much does money count?

These questions are legitimate, especially since, in Illinois, there are no limits on who can make campaign contributions and how much any individual or entity can kick in. In other states, and for federal elections, there are limits and restrictions. But not here. On top of that, up until the late 1990s, Illinois had a deplorable system of making campaign finance data available to the public. In fact, it would have been hard to purposely design a better system for keeping campaign finance data away from the public. So the money rules for Illinois evolved as part of a game played by professional politicians in front of few — if any — spectators. Add a political scandal or two, and it's no wonder citizens, the news media, and even some participants question the extent to which cash corrupts the workings of Illinois state politics.

A political scientist at the state capital of Springfield is a kid at a funhouse arcade with a bottomless pocketful of change. Every stripe of political posturing and public policymaking is everywhere all the time. There is so much action, so much activity. It may be fascinating or frightening, but it is never dull. Having spent four years working on a legislative staff in the late 1970s and then moving to Sangamon State University (now the University of Illinois at Springfield) to run the Illinois Legislative Staff Intern Program and teach political studies, my professional and personal interests for the past 25 years have remained focused on the Illinois General Assembly. "Follow the money" has always been sound advice for private detectives and students of politics. Taking an interest in the role that money plays in Illinois politics and taking advantage of new technologies to study that role are natural things for a Springfield-based political scientist to do.

Since 1990, I have been building a database of campaign contributions and expenditures for legislative candidates, constitutional officers, and the two state political parties. Once the data from the 1999-2000 election cycle is completely integrated, the contribution table alone will exceed 400,000 records for more than 700 candidates. The time and effort involved in data entry, standardization, and coding for a database of this size is staggering. (If I'd have known in 1990 what a cruel taskmaster this database would become, I might have studied comparative legislative committee systems instead.) And then, after creating and organizing the data, I came to the inevitable question: "What now?"

For me the "what now" falls into three related, but separate tasks.

First is the very important job of providing, as completely as possible, a descriptive and accurate picture of where the money in Illinois politics comes from, who gets it, and what they do with it. Citizens, the news media, advocacy groups, interest groups, politicians, and academic researchers should have free and easy access to this information. An objective, accurate foundation is essential to any discussion about the role that money does or should play within Illinois politics.

Second is to analyze the role of money and how it affects the outcomes of the Illinois political system. Studying Illinois provides insight into the way that money influences elections and shapes public policy and into the strategic decisions of interest groups, corporations, individuals, political leaders, and candidates. At a more general level, studying Illinois provides a strong indication of what the impact would be of a complete deregulation of campaign finance in another state or at the federal level.

Third is to become active in the political process itself. Describing and analyzing are widely accepted roles for a political scientist. But a political scientist is also a citizen. As citizens, we all have at least a civic obligation to participate in the political process. But beyond participation, we have an obligation to engage in it. Making politics more accessible, open, comprehensible, meaningful, and responsible should always be the goal of a democratic society. For the political scientist who studies campaign finance, there is a special obligation toward advocacy.

The goal of studying campaign finance and then engaging in the process led *Illinois Issues* publisher Ed Wojcicki and me to Larry Hansen, the vice president of The Joyce Foundation. Larry's vision and leadership within The Joyce Foundation resulted in its support for a program area dealing with campaign finance issues in the Midwest. Through Joyce, Ed and I helped create the Illinois Campaign Finance Project. Besides basic research, the heart of the project was a blue-ribbon task force chaired by former U.S. Senator Paul Simon and former Illinois Governor William Stratton. The task force was charged with making recommendations about campaign finance in Illinois. Its final report, *Tainted Democracy*, was issued in 1997.

A key member of that task force was Cindi Canary, the former head of the League of Women Voters of Illinois. With the support of The Joyce Foundation, Cindi formed the Illinois Campaign for Political Reform, a coalition of advocacy and public interest groups seeking to change the way that Illinois regulates campaign finance. With continued support from Larry Hansen and The Joyce Foundation, I set up the Sunshine Project at the University of Illinois at Springfield in 1997 to provide research and analysis for groups such as the Illinois Campaign for Political Reform as well as citizens, politicians, and members of the news media.

Money Counts is, for me, the next step toward informing, analyzing, and engaging.

Looking back over my time in Springfield, it is striking how Illinois state government and Illinois politics and the forces that drive them have changed. State government, as a whole, has become more professional and more meaningful to the lives of Illinois citizens. What the state does and how it does it is almost unrecognizable from the perspective of Illinois state government in the early 1960s. The 1990s devolution of power from the federal government to the states was made possible, in part, by the incredible upgrading of the institutions of state government that took place between the late 1960s and the early 1980s.

But much of what else has changed in Illinois politics is not positive. Political parties are weaker, legislators are less independent, interest groups are more powerful, political campaigns have become more sophisticated and much more expensive, and the decision-making processes have become much more centralized. In the middle of this political universe are the legislative leaders and the governor. And the core of their power is money.

This book explores the money-driven nature of state politics. Chapter 1 will introduce you to the state's evolving political culture.

You'll see why money counts for so much and why those in power are in no hurry to change that fact. Chapter 2 looks at the history of Illinois' campaign finance laws, what the laws do and do not cover, and the recent changes that have been adopted. It also compares Illinois' approach to regulating the role of money in politics to other states and the federal system.

The money that fuels Illinois politics begins as private money. Chapter 3 traces the way that money from individuals, corporations, unions, professional associations, and interest groups flows into the system. Who gives the most and to whom they give tell us a good deal about the nature of the political system. The same is true of the list of those who don't give. As you'll see in Chapters 4 and 5, all of this has implications for the outcome of elections and the policies that are approved by the legislature and signed into law by the governor.

Chapter 6 addresses both the certain future of doing nothing and the uncertain future of reform. It presents a blueprint for a strategy of incremental change while keeping the door open for the scandal-driven opportunities for more rapid and dramatic change that will inevitably arise.

Changing the money rules, which by now are ingrained deeply in the Illinois political culture, is not something done overnight. It takes patience, thought, and faith. It requires an understanding of how things are, how they came to be, what they could be, and what they ought to be. I hope *Money Counts* stirs you to action; that it makes you more aware of state government and the influences upon it; that it causes you to attend town meetings and to ask questions of your elected officials; that it encourages you contribute to causes you believe in and work for change. I know that's a lot to ask of one small book. But the only way to make our government truly representative of *all* the people of the state of Illinois is to change the current money system one citizen and one candidate at a time.

Acknowledgments

While any errors of fact, omission, or interpretation are mine alone, the combined efforts of many people have contributed to any value this book has in advancing the dialogue on the role of money in Illinois politics.

I am deeply indebted to Larry Hansen, Cindi Canary, and Ed Wojcicki for their moral support, intellectual guidance, and friendship. Without the continued financial support of The Joyce Foundation, only a small portion of the research and analysis produced over the past six years would have been possible. It is literally not possible to overstate the role that Larry Hansen and The Joyce Foundation have played in bringing the issue of money and politics to the public agenda in Illinois.

Rupert Borgsmiller and Ron Michaelson of the State Board of Elections provided technical assistance and guidance through the maze of campaign finance data and campaign finance regulation. Charles Wheeler III, director of the Public Affairs Reporting Program at the University of Illinois at Springfield, and an acknowledged human repository of Illinois political history, looked at some of these chapters and offered his helpful advice.

The University of Illinois at Springfield has provided a home and a safe haven for my research, writing, and advocacy. First David Everson and then Jack Van Der Slik in their roles as director of the Illinois Legislative Studies Center provided the organizational support and intellectual guidance necessary to sustain my projects at the university.

Rodd Whelpley, Beverley Scobell, Janelle Bandy, Diana Nelson, and the rest of the staff at Institute Publications edited the text and transformed unorganized and incomplete writing into a professional, readable book. And the fact that you are holding a copy of it in your hands attests to the wonderful job that communications consultant Jim Bray has done promoting *Money Counts*.

Finally, the joy and satisfaction of producing a book are private matters that are difficult to share with your family, while the strain, stress, and frustration are all too easy to share. Janet, Jenny, Alicia, and Renee endured them with grace and understanding, and I am grateful for their support.

List of Abbreviations

ABDI — Associated Beer Distributors of Illinois

AFL-CIO — American Federation of Labor - Congress of Industrial Organizations

AFSCME — American Federation of State, County and Municipal Employees

ComEd — Commonwealth Edison

FEC — Federal Election Commission

IEA — Illinois Education Association

IFT — Illinois Federation of Teachers

IHHA — Illinois Hospital and HealthSystems Association

IMA — Illinois Manufacturers' Association

ISLA — Illinois Small Loan Association

IVI-IPO — Independent Voters of Illinois - Independent Precinct Organizations

MSI — Management Services of Illinois, Inc.

PAC — Political Action Committee

RPAC — Illinois Association of Realtors Political Action Committee

TIP — Hotel Employees and Restaurant Employees International Union Tip Education Fund

WSDI — Wine and Spirits Distributors of Illinois

Winning Ugly

Cash
and the
Political Culture
of Illinois

The ultimate symbol of money in Illinois politics is a shoe box. Even though it has been decades since the death of Secretary of State Paul Powell in 1970, and the subsequent discovery of more than $800,000 in cash in his hotel room, the image of that tattered box endures.

Powell was the "gray fox of Vienna," three-time speaker of the Illinois House of Representatives, a deal maker extraordinaire. As a public servant, he never made an annual salary of more than $30,000 from a career in elected office that lasted nearly 35 years. Those outside of Illinois politics may have been shocked to discover that Powell died with all that cash and an estate valued at more than $2.6 million (Hartley 1999). But those on the inside had known for a long while that in the Land of Lincoln, money can drive politics and politics can drive money.

The playing field in 1970 was remarkably wide open. In keeping with the political culture of the time, laws regulating campaign finance, lobbying, and political ethics were so weak and unenforced that they were virtually nonexistent. There were no restrictions on giving money or other gifts to elected officials and no restrictions on what elected officials did with them. Bribery, extortion, theft, and fraud were crimes then as now. But the subtle and not-so-subtle ways that private money and public power intertwined to distort and corrupt the political process were unabated by laws or public scrutiny. Robert Hartley's biography of Powell, published in 1999, focused new attention on his career and the times in which he lived. A comforting thought would be that Paul Powell and his shoe box represent a different era in Illinois politics, "a long time ago and far, far away." The truth is that Powell's politics and his ethics would fit nicely in Illinois' current political culture.

Illinois is the home of a strong tradition of highly moral public servants stretching from Abraham Lincoln to Adlai Stevenson, Paul Douglas, and, more recently, Paul Simon. Paul Powell is representative of a different (but concurrent) political tradition in Illinois politics — a tradition of power politics and public corruption. There has always been this unfortunate downside to the importance of money in Illinois politics: the ease with which it flows into the process and the easy virtue that pervades the attitudes of professional politicians and well-heeled private interests. Augustus French, the state's ninth governor, was already acting on tradition when, in the 1840s, he joined the rush to buy cheap government land along projected railroad lines and then tried to influence the legislature to grant charters to companies that would make his investments pay off (Howard 1999). In 1973, former Governor Otto Kerner was convicted on bribery and income tax evasion charges when a jury found that he bought racetrack stock at bargain prices from horse racing mogul Marjorie Lindheimer Everett, granted her political favors, and then sold the stock back to her at a profit (Howard 1999). And, in 1996, after an investigation into his alleged involvement in an embezzlement scheme involving the U.S. House Post Office, Illinois congressman and longtime chairman of the House Ways and Means Committee, Dan Rostenkowski, went to federal prison. He had plea-bargained down to a conviction on mail fraud (Merriner 1999).

It is true that the legal framework of Illinois politics changed significantly from 1970 to 2000 and with it the ethical climate as well. Personal corruption is less prevalent and no longer accepted with the shrug and the wink of Powell's era. (Kerner and Rostenkowski did time, after all.) But Powell is hardly an anachronism, even in the Illinois politics of today. In 1994, on a highway near Milwaukee, an unqualified Illinois truck driver named Ricardo Guzman caused an accident that killed six children. Investigation into how Guzman obtained his license touched off a federal investigation into a bribes-for-licenses scheme that implicated five Chicago-area secretary of state testing facilities. By April 15, 2000, Operation Safe Road, as the ongoing investigation was called, had secured 25 guilty pleas. Former secretary of state employees admitted that they funneled over $170,000 in bribe money into then-Secretary of State George Ryan's campaign fund (*Illinois Issues* 2000). Ryan won the governorship in 1998, before the investigation had gathered its momentum. He subsequently denied knowledge of his employees' illegal activities, and, by May 2000, had donated $200,000 from his campaign coffers to charity, a gesture apparently designed to show he was purging tainted money from his accounts.

Personal ethics aside, what about Powell, the politician? How would he do in modern Illinois politics? Until recently, the answer certainly would have been, "Quite well." From 1970 to 1997, the only substantive changes in the official rules of the game of money and politics were a reporting and disclosure law passed in 1976. That law covered the contribution and expenditure of campaign funds, and in 1993 a lobbyist registration and expenditure reporting law passed. Even these changes were weak laws with grossly underfunded agencies providing minimal oversight and enforcement.

What about more recent changes? The years 1997 and 1998 were, by Illinois standards, a period of remarkable reform. The state now mandates electronic disclosure of campaign contributions and expenditures, with increased details on where contributions come from. Candidates' reports are posted on the State Board of Elections' web site. There is a ban on using campaign funds for personal use, along with other ethics reforms. There are much stronger lobbying registration and reporting requirements, a ban on gifts to public officials, and greatly enhanced competitive bidding regulations for government contracts. The press is more attentive, more knowledgeable, and more aggressive in reporting the role that money plays in Illinois politics. The success of these efforts has energized and empowered public interest groups pushing for more sweeping reforms. Looking forward in early 1997, most of the changes that have become law looked impossible. By 1999, the momentum had clearly shifted. Surely the day is near when we can confidently say that Powell's politics as well as his ethics are hopelessly out of place in Illinois politics. Or is it?

Illinois politicians spent a record $91 million running for the legislature, governor, and the other five constitutional officers elected in 1998 (those officers being lieutenant governor, attorney general, secretary of state, treasurer, and comptroller). Governor George Ryan spent more than $13 million getting elected. For the General Assembly, each election features only a few highly competitive, hyperexpensive contests. These "targeted" races are scripted and financed largely by the four legislative leaders (the speaker of the House, the House minority leader, the Senate president, and the

Senate minority leader). In 1998, spending topped $1 million in two Senate races and $850,000 in two House races. The legislative leaders provided more than 60 percent of the funding for those contests. The legislative leaders are free (as they always have been) to raise as much as they can and spend as much as they want on behalf of their chosen candidates for seats in the legislature. But money from the party leadership never gets spread very thin because the vast majority of legislative races are over before they start, with well-funded, well-known incumbents facing little or no opposition. Those taking on an incumbent without assistance from a legislative leader are unable to attract financial support beyond their families and friends. With so many lopsided races, is it any wonder that people stay away from the polls in droves?

Citizen apathy leaves the political field open to special interests. In the heyday of Paul Powell and Otto Kerner, horse track owners tied the knot between campaign money and favorable legislation. Today, the state's gambling industry includes riverboat casinos. A small number of gambling interests contributed more than $1.9 million to legislators and constitutional officers in 1997 and 1998. They followed up with more than $900,000 in contributions in 1999. In that year, a major gambling bill extended riverboat gambling to Cook County and allowed those casinos to operate without cruising. The measure also gave racetrack owners tax breaks and direct state subsidies based on a percentage of the revenues generated by the Cook County boat. The bill passed the legislature and was signed into law by the governor (Simpson 1999a). Was this an isolated incident? No. That same legislative session, Chicago Blackhawks owner and liquor distributor William Wirtz was a major proponent of a bill that would require liquor suppliers to give three months' notice and provide justification before bowing out of contracts with their current distributors. Interests supporting the Wirtz bill contributed more than $300,000 to legislative and constitutional officer candidates in 1998 and 1999. Wirtz also hired lobbyists who contributed more than $300,000 on their own during the same period. The General Assembly passed the protectionist legislation for both the liquor and soda pop distributors in the spring of

1999, even though the Federal Trade Commission called the measures anticompetitive. Governor Ryan signed the legislation as soon as it hit his desk, and the law took effect immediately (Simpson 1999b). So, in 1999, we see that large campaign contributions and highly paid lobbyists drove issues that had little public support but huge financial implications for their supporters. Why? Because there are still no limits on how much groups, corporations, and individuals can contribute to the political funds of candidates. People with the most money don't always win in Illinois, either in the legislature or at the ballot box. But they almost always beat those without money in both arenas.

A stark reality of Illinois politics at the turn of this century is the overwhelming political power amassed by the legislative leaders. Their control over legislative elections and the policy process in the legislature is almost total, and it rests, to a significant degree, on their unrestricted ability to raise and spend campaign contributions. No clearer example of the exercise and the consequences of the leaders' power exists than the $49 billion state budget rubber-stamped by the legislature in April 2000. The budget was almost exclusively a product of negotiations among the four legislative leaders and the governor. It was brought forth and ratified in a single day. The individual policy decisions embodied in the spending decisions were not debated in committee or on the floor of the House or Senate. To say that the rank-and-file members of the legislature were largely irrelevant to the process would be an understatement. The four leaders buried more than $250 million in lump sum appropriations in the budget to be used for funding pork projects at their discretion. That discretion only tightens the vise grip leaders have on the rank-and-file members of each chamber.

So, in spite of changes in campaign finance and ethics laws, in spite of the best efforts of good government groups to reform the system during the last 30 years of the twentieth century, the essence of Illinois politics has not changed. Ours is still a politics in which the pursuit of winning and power and jobs and clout usually prevail over principles and policy and ideals. One of the tools of this type of politics is money. The rules of the political game still favor those outside of government who have money and know how to use it. Within government, those who are willing and able to use their power and position to raise money enjoy the same advantage. In spite of recent reforms, Illinois still has the most wide-open, unrestricted campaign finance system in the nation.

Political power is concentrated in the hands of legislative leaders and the governor in ways that Powell could only imagine. Paul Powell was a leader with a well-deserved reputation for making deals and raising money. As a politician, he would not just survive in our current politics. He would thrive.

Illinois' Political Culture

What is it about politics in Illinois? Is it an accident that the two most important U.S. Supreme Court decisions limiting political patronage, *Elrod v. Burns* and *Rutan v. The Republican Party of Illinois*, addressed cases from Illinois? Could legendary Chicago Mayor Richard J. Daley have built the same invincible political machine in Milwaukee or Denver of the 1950s and 1960s? Why is Illinois considered the Wild West of campaign finance?

To begin to answer some of these questions, first finish this sentence: "Politics is ..." If you answered "Politics is the noble pursuit of the public good that enriches both society and the individual," you are probably not from Illinois. If you answered, "Politics is a dirty business," you may well have grown up in the Land of Lincoln.

Illinois has a specific, dominant political culture. Culture is the totality of learned beliefs about the nature of institutions and human relationships within a society. Political culture is the totality of learned beliefs about the nature of political institutions and political relationships. Political culture both reflects and shapes the behaviors, institutions, and relationships through which collective, public decisions are made for a community, city, state, or nation. A politics that functions with the belief that politics is a business, and inherently a dirty business, will produce vastly different institutions and behaviors from one that functions with the belief that politics is the noble pursuit of activities for the public good that enriches both society and the individual.

Political scientist Daniel Elazar has sketched out two competing traditions within American politics. In the first, the political system is seen as "a marketplace in which the primary public relationships are products of bargaining between individuals and groups acting primarily out of self-interest" (Elazar 1996, xxi). In the second, the political system is seen as a commonwealth "in which the whole people have an undivided interest and the citizens cooperate in an effort to create and maintain the best government in order to implement certain shared moral principles" (Elazar 1996, xxi). Elazar identified different political cultures that he felt characterized how the basic differences in ways that the tension between the two traditions were resolved in politics. He also identified particular areas or states in which each of these cultures were dominant. What Elazar called "individualistic" political culture is the most useful in explaining Illinois politics, although there is a strong strain of "moralistic" political culture as well.

Elazar used the term "individualistic" for political cultures in which concerns for the marketplace dominate concerns for the commonwealth. Illinois has long been considered the prototype of a state with primarily an individualistic political culture. In fact, in their book *Illinois Politics and Government* (1996), respected Illinois political scientists Samuel Gove and James Nowlan use the concept of individualistic political culture as a central theme to explain the development and practice of Illinois politics.

In the individualistic political culture, the purpose of government is to protect private interests and provide the services demanded by the people. There is no public interest beyond the aggregate expression of individual self-interests. At a meeting I attended in Speaker Michael Madigan's office in the spring of 1989, a former Illinois mayor turned lobbyist said, "Where I come from, good government is five votes on a Tuesday night." It was the quintessential expression of individualistic political culture.

In the individualistic political culture, politics is a business like any other business within society. It competes for talent with every other business. It is a profession in which individuals can succeed and thereby improve themselves. As such, the best players are professionals, and amateurs are held in low esteem. When I started working for the legislature in the middle 1970s, legislators, particularly those representing Chicago and the Cook County regular Democratic organization, often derided the League of Women Voters and good government reform groups as "the plague of women voters" and the "goo goos." For those legislators, politics wasn't a hobby you played at in your spare time in the pursuit of principles. Politics was a job. It was about winning and losing — not principles. Those attitudes about participation extended to voting. For those running Democratic or Republican county political machines, perfect election day weather was an early November snowstorm — or at least a cold, driving rain. The pros knew they could get their people to the polls. Amateurs would likely stay home. Those same attitudes about who should participate in the business of Illinois politics and why still prevail in the minds of Illinois' professional politicos.

In an individualistic political culture, politics is primarily about winning power, controlling jobs, and gaining financial advantage. Policy is important, but it often plays a secondary role in support of the struggle for power and advantage. For these reasons, change of any kind is difficult to achieve in an individualistic-minded state like Illinois. People and groups with power climbed up the ladder of political success under the existing system. Regardless of how they feel about the nature of that political system, they know how to win. Changes in the process mean risks and uncertain outcomes. When it comes to policy, the tendency is to say, "I have to find out where the people are going so I can lead them." Raising issues that are not on the public radar or pushing policy changes that run counter to public opinion are risky behaviors for politicians whose primary concerns are staying in office and retaining power. Individualistic political culture produces a politics in which emerging policy problems are dealt with through inaction and policy imitation rather than action and innovation. Welfare reform is just one of the latest in a whole host of policy areas where Illinois was not a leader in adopting fundamental change. A wait-and-see attitude to public policy produces few mistakes and fewer breakthroughs, but protection of the status quo is generally a safe bet for those who hold the reins of power.

In fact, the idea that those who win and serve in politics have a right to expect some advantage from the political system is central to the idea of an individualistic political culture. Politics is a business with equal opportunity to run and win. But, it is a business with limited financial rewards and low social esteem. In order to attract and keep people, there is, in an individualistic culture, widespread acceptance that those in government will be able to reap some private benefit from public service. At the extreme, there is the long list of political scandals and public officials convicted for corruption in office. But, in practice, a certain level of corruption is expected and tolerated as a cost of the system. Professional politicians have had to develop their own sense of how much the public will bear. But, as an old Chicago adage warns: "Pigs get fat. Hogs get butchered."

Carl Sandburg pegged Chicago the "hog butcher for the world." It likely would not surprise Illinois' poet laureate that the state's troubled history of corruption in public employment and public contracts has reached into the twenty-first century. In the individualistic political culture, public agencies function to provide both the services that the public demands and jobs for those who support the elected officials who control the political system. Political scientist John Fenton characterizes such states as Illinois as having job-oriented political systems as opposed to such states as Wisconsin that have policy-oriented systems (Fenton 1966). Illinois has long been considered a classic patronage state at all levels of government. In *Elrod v. Burns*, 427 U.S. 347 (1976), the U.S. Supreme Court declared it unconstitutional for Cook County Sheriff Richard Elrod to fire employees because they had voted in Republican primary elections. In *Rutan v. Republican Party of Illinois*, 110 S Ct. 2734 (1990), the U.S. Supreme Court declared that the administration of Illinois Governor Jim Thompson acted unconstitutionally when it hired people for state jobs based on their participation in Republican primary elections and support for Republican candidates. Have these decisions reversed the impact of Illinois political culture on public employment practices? They certainly have driven patronage underground, but reports of its death may prove to be greatly exaggerated. In fact, "pinstripe patronage," the granting of political favors to business people, has now largely replaced the county bosses' handing out jobs as was done in an earlier era.

In the late winter and early spring of 2000, a raft of newspaper stories alleged political favoritism involving campaign contributions and building leases in the secretary of state's office and no-bid public contracts and sweetheart deals in the mayor's office in Chicago. Whatever the merits of these particular charges, they were consistent with a long history of linking public business to campaign contributions. (In cases where the link between contributions and public business is absolute, newspapers have no qualms about using the word "bribery.")

The role of money in Illinois politics is a perfect reflection of its individualistic nature. The wide-open, largely unrestricted campaign finance system is a product of the culture, and it enhances and protects the culture. The free flow of money between private and public sectors in Illinois provides maximum opportunity for those with power to use money to keep power. The system also allows those seeking power to use money to gain power. The history of regulating the flow of money into Illinois politics is a history of putting forth the absolute least effort necessary and of keeping the issue off the public agenda in order to retain the advantages that the free flow of money provides for incumbent public officials, those seeking office, and private interests with money. Those with power in Illinois politics tend to be politicians and groups who embrace Illinois' political culture. They are experts at using the existing campaign finance system to retain their positions of power. From this perspective, campaign finance reform is always assessed first in terms of political advantage rather than in terms of the public good.

While the individualistic culture dominates Illinois, there is a strong undercurrent of what Elazar calls the moralistic culture. In most ways, moralistic political culture is the opposite of individualistic political culture. The emphasis is on politics as a means to advance the common good. The focus is on policies and ideas.

Ideology is more important and political parties less important than in the individualistic political culture. The widest possible participation is encouraged, not only because it produces a politics of shared values and goals, but also because participation is a right and a duty that enriches the individual. Illinois' moralistic underpinning can be seen at the local level in Chicago's long-standing conflict between the regular Democratic Party organizations and the IVI-IPO (Independent Voters of Illinois - Independent Precinct Organizations). More recently, the moralistic culture is evident at the state level in the politics of former Senator Paul Simon and former Congressman John Anderson.

These moralistic rumblings notwithstanding, campaign finance reformers in Illinois must assume that they will operate in an idividualistic political culture. The reaction of the general public to politics in a state with an individualistic political culture is one of disinterest, disengagement, contempt, and mistrust. Those who do not participate or participate only occasionally have learned from their parents, friends, teachers, churches, and the news media that politics is a dirty business. It is something other people do. All politicians and all political parties are the same and all of them are corrupt. Nothing ever changes, and the little guy never wins. Given the attitudes of the politicians and the Illinois public, the lack of progress in achieving change in the political system and the lack of enthusiasm for change come as no surprise.

Campaign Finance Reform and the Future of Illinois Politics

Money is not the root of all that is evil in Illinois politics. But the way it flows into and through the system facilitates the existing process and reinforces the prevailing political culture. To many inside and outside the process, Illinois is a poster child for campaign finance reform. Whatever the problem — personal corruption, state contracts for campaign contributions, incumbent election advantage, hyperexpensive targeted legislative races, the power of legislative leaders, the centralization of power in the hands of the governor and the four legislative leaders, special interests dominating in the legislature — the answer is campaign finance reform.

But, are the problems in the Illinois political process that flow from the role of money imagined, or are they real? If real, what will happen if the political system remains as it is? What about change? Would any reform in our campaign finance system have a major impact on the policies we adopt and the general nature of our politics? Can we make Illinois elections more competitive and less dependent on legislative leaders and powerful interest groups? Can we level the playing field in the legislature, either by restraining some interests or empowering others? Is any change possible when those who benefit most from the status quo hold the keys to adopting any reform? Finally, is campaign finance reform worth it?

Our campaign finance laws did not create the political culture. Rather, the laws (or lack thereof) were created to reflect and serve the culture, making the free flow of money into and within the political system possible. The current system is a powerful tool in the hands of the legislative leaders and the governor. The interest groups that dominate the policy process have used the campaign finance system to take maximum advantage of their financial resources. The Illinois Constitution prohibits ordinary citizens from changing or making state laws through the initiative process. But how can we change the culture without changing the laws? And without changing the culture, how can we get those in power to make any new laws work? The challenge is somehow to change the laws in order to change the culture and change the culture in order to change the laws. While any attempt at political reform faces a "Catch 22," the dilemma when it comes to Illinois politics is particularly binding.

Events, often in the form of political scandals, can provide opportunities for ambitious changes in the Illinois political system. A desire to address an outrage can suspend business as usual and put questions about the political power structure and its processes on the table. Unfortunately, in the wake of a scandal, it is the people in power who take full blame for their malfeasance, and the systemic problems concerning the basic nature of Illinois go largely unexamined. "Throwing the rascals out" may be both justified and satisfying, but it is not a formula for political change.

Preparing to take advantage of a scandal is a worthy action, as would be mounting a full-scale frontal assault on the political system. But these are also problematic strategies for change. The "right" scandal may not happen. Proposals for radical change will never survive the current political process. But we must do something.

There is a solution and a strategy to the campaign finance problem in Illinois. The solution is to change the political culture, however resistant it is to change. The strategy is more complicated. The following chapters will detail the breadth and depth to which money rules the Illinois political system. With an understanding of that context, it should become clear that we must change the laws and the culture. As you will see in Chapter 6, change is possible, but the best strategy is one of modest steps that cumulatively, almost unnoticeably, become giant leaps.

Trying to Tame the Wild West

Regulating Campaign Finance in Illinois

W hen it comes to campaign finance, Illinois has a well-deserved reputation as a no-holds-barred, take-no-prisoners, free-for-all ethical swamp. References to Illinois as the "Wild West of campaign finance" strike home with citizens and political players alike. Before 1999, it was almost impossible — short of refusing to file disclosure reports — to violate Illinois campaign finance law. For example, a representative of Illinois Widgets, Incorporated could have met a candidate for county coroner on the steps of the state Capitol and given her a $1 billion campaign contribution. The county coroner candidate could have given $200 million each to the governor, the speaker of the House, and the state Senate president; spent $200 million on her own campaign; and used the remaining $200 million to build a house, buy a car, play the stock market, and throw a hell of a party. But, under new ethical restrictions, which took effect on January 1, 1999, the $1 billion contribution could no longer take place on state property, and none of it could be converted to personal use. So the car, the house, and the online trading are out, but the party is probably still on if it involves campaign workers or constituent relations. And unlimited transfers of money from one political campaign to another are still allowed.

From the perspective of the inaction from 1973 to 1998, recent successes in changing Illinois campaign finance law are certainly encouraging. But news of the death of Illinois' wide-open system of campaign finance is certainly premature.

The Recent History
of State Campaign Finance Regulations

The modern era of state regulation of campaign contributions and expenditures is rooted in the Watergate scandal. The primary focus of the congressional and media investigations was the question of obstruction of justice and abuse of power by President Richard Nixon. But, revelations about the amount of money raised for Nixon's 1972 re-election campaign and the way money was raised and spent sparked renewed interest in establishing a tough federal law regulating contributions and expenditures in federal elections. That law, the 1974 amendments to the Federal Election Campaign Act, provided strict limits on campaign contributions and expenditures in federal elections and a system of public funding for presidential elections.

At the same time, there was a flurry of activity at the state level, as state legislators reacted to public criticism of the role of money in the electoral process. From 1973 to 1975, most states either strengthened existing laws regulating campaign finance or enacted them for the first time. Many state laws mirrored the federal law in providing limits on who could contribute to candidates and how much they could contribute. The laws also set limits on how much a candidate could spend or how much could be spent by others in support of a candidate (Alexander 1992; Sorauf 1988). Illinois, however, adopted only a minimal reporting and disclosure law. The new law placed no restrictions on spending, no restrictions on who could contribute, and no restrictions on how much they could contribute. It also contained no public funding for campaigns.

The reform movement engendered by Watergate proved to be short-lived. In 1976, the United States Supreme Court invalidated large portions of the 1974 amendments to the federal election law with its ruling in *Buckley v. Valeo*, 424 U.S. 1 (1976). The court ruled that the requirements that campaign contributions be reported and disclosed and that limits on how much a person or group can contribute to a candidate are constitutional. But the court also held that limits on how much a candidate can spend on behalf of his or her own election are unconstitutional. Likewise, limits on how much a person or group can spend independently on behalf of a candidate were also held to be unconstitutional violations of free speech.

Congress was forced to revise federal election law to bring it into compliance with *Buckley*. Since the Supreme Court's ruling also extended to the states through the Fourteenth Amendment, the decision also defined what states can and cannot do in restricting the flow of money into political campaigns. By extension, the ruling defined how the states could and could not restrict spending by candidates and others in support of candidates. While many states had to adopt significant changes in their campaign finance laws to bring them into compliance with the ruling in *Buckley,* no changes were required in Illinois' law.

The constitutional framework for regulating campaign finance at the federal and state level is still controlled by the logic of *Buckley*.

Constitutional Limits on Regulating Campaign Finance

Prior to the *Buckley* decision, it was widely assumed that laws regulating campaign contributions and expenditures represented a legitimate governmental interest in protecting the integrity of the electoral process. The United States Supreme Court ruling upholding federal election laws had relied on arguments to that effect. The major decision prior to *Buckley*, *Burroughs v. U.S.*, 290 U.S. 534, was decided in 1934. When the 1974 changes in the federal election law were challenged in court in 1975, a federal appellate court upheld the changes. The lower courts accepted the arguments of the proponents of the law: that this was an area that could be regulated by legislative action because of the need to protect the electoral process from the corrupting and distorting impact of money.

In deciding *Buckley*, the court considered four basic aspects of campaign finance: (1) mandatory spending limits, (2) contribution limits, (3) disclosure requirements, and (4) public funding and voluntary spending limits.

The Supreme Court held that giving a campaign contribution to a candidate and campaign spending by a candidate or on behalf of a candidate is political speech, a form of free speech protected by the First Amendment to the U.S. Constitution. Having held that campaign contributions and expenditures are protected forms of speech, the court then considered what, if any, restrictions Congress might legitimately place on them. The court rejected the idea that there was a legitimate legislative interest in preserving the integrity of the electoral process that would justify placing limits on the rights of individuals to engage in political speech through campaign expenditures. As such, the court held that there was no legitimate legislative interest in limiting expenditures on political campaigns, either by candidates themselves or by others acting independently of the candidate they are supporting. Following that logic, the court struck down federal limits on campaign expenditures by candidates and by others acting in support of candidates as unconstitutional limits on free speech.

In considering the issues of contribution limits and public disclosure, the court found that there was a legitimate legislative interest in preventing corruption or the appearance of corruption of the political process. By corruption, the justices were referring to the exchange of a campaign contribution for a favorable action by a public official or by a candidate once elected, a *quid pro quo*. As such, the court upheld limits on how much an individual, group, or political party committee can contribute to a candidate for public office. Because reporting and disclosure are essential to determining what relationship exists between contributors and candidates, the court also upheld requirements that candidates report the sources and amounts of the contributions they accept and the expenditures they make. In addition, candidates must make those reports available to the general public.

Finally, on the issue of public funding and voluntary spending limits, the court upheld public funding of presidential campaigns and the requirement that candidates accept voluntary spending limits as a condition for receiving public funds.

All of the significant campaign finance decisions handed down by the Supreme Court since 1976 have applied the reasoning of *Buckley*. In *First National Bank v. Bellotti*, 435 U.S.765 (1978), the Supreme Court examined the question of what limits can be placed on contributions by corporations toward state public policy referendums and initiatives, types of elections where there is no candidate. The court held that prohibitions on participation by corporate entities were unconstitutional because the absence of a candidate for a public office eliminated any possibility of a *quid pro quo*. In *Federal Election Commission v. National Conservative Political Action Committee*, 470 U.S. 480 (1985), the court struck down a limit on independent expenditures by political action committees (PACs) in support of candidates. In *Federal Election Commission v. Massachusetts Citizens for Life*, 107 S.Ct. 616 (1986), the court invalidated a federal prohibition on direct corporate activities in elections as they applied to nonstock corporations formed entirely to pursue policy goals while leaving the general prohibition on direct corporate activity in candidate elections in place. In *Austin v. Michigan State Chamber of Commerce*, 494 U.S. 652 (1990), the U.S. Supreme Court upheld a state law prohibiting corporations from making expenditures in support of state candidates. A majority of the court held that such expenditures could result in the corruption — or at least in the appearance of corruption — of the political process. In *Colorado Republican Federal Campaign Committee v. Federal Election Commission*, 116 S.Ct. 2309 (1996), the U.S. Supreme Court held that political parties could make independent expenditures on behalf of candidates and that those expenditures could not be regulated.

The constitutional status of "issue ads" (ads which tie a candidate to an issue position) is unclear. However, the majority of federal circuit courts that have ruled on cases involving issue ads have followed the reasoning of the First Circuit Court. That court held that issue advocacy or issue ads may not be regulated unless they cross the line into expressed election advocacy by specifically urging the defeat or election of a candidate or urging votes for or against a specific candidates (see *Faucher v. Federal Election Commission*, 928 F.2d 468 (1991)). Federal legislation requiring disclosure by groups funding issue ads was signed into law in the summer of 2000. The constitutionality of those requirements has not been determined.

In general, the United States Supreme Court has upheld contribution limits against a variety of legal challenges. In a recent case from Missouri, *Nixon v. Shrink,* No. 98-963 (2000), the Supreme Court by a six-to-three decision reaffirmed the core of *Buckley* by upholding the constitutionality of contribution limits against a challenge that they placed a burden on the exercise of protected speech. But the court tries to be practical in this limitation. It has struck down state contribution-limit thresholds that it considered too low to provide all candidates with an opportunity to participate in the process.

The legal status of political action committees at the federal level flows from an advisory opinion of the Federal Election Commission

(FEC) in 1975, which upheld the Sun Oil Company organization's right to solicit campaign contributions from its employees (Federal Election Commission 1975). The basic rule is that a corporation or union can spend general funds to establish and administer a political action committee whose purpose is to contribute to federal candidates even though the corporation or union is prohibited from making contributions to federal candidates. Congress could prohibit PACs, but it has chosen not to.

Federal law places a limit on contributions to political parties if the funds are used to support the election of federal candidates. There is no limit on contributions to political parties if the funds are used for "party building" and voter registration activities. Money that falls under contribution limits is called "hard" money. Money that is not subject to contribution limits is called "soft" money. The controversy at the federal level is over what constitutes party-building activities. Advocates of soft-money bans contend that issue ads and independent expenditures by political parties, which are funded by soft money, have made contribution limits meaningless. But, soft money is a political rather than a constitutional question. Congress could eliminate soft money by placing all contributions to political parties under the current contribution limits.

Types of Campaign Finance Laws:
Sunshine, Sticks, and Carrots

Even within the restrictions of the *Buckley* decision, state and local election authorities have adopted a wide range of campaign finance laws. The broad choices are the sunshine option, the stick option, and the carrot-and-stick option.

Systems that rely solely on reporting and disclosure to ensure money will not be used to unduly influence elections or public policy are called sunshine systems. The sunshine option rests on three assumptions. First, left to their own devices, contributors and politicians will use money to their advantage in both elections and policymaking. Second, with complete disclosure and reporting of where the money comes from and where it goes, the public and the press will take notice of where money is coming from and where it is being spent. And third, the fear of public and press attention will cause both contributors and politicians to modify their behavior in ways that will reduce to acceptable levels the role of money in elections and policymaking. At a minimum, all 50 states and the federal system have basic sunshine requirements and mechanisms in place.

Campaign finance systems that try to limit the influence of money on elections and policy by placing restrictions on the flow of money are stick systems. Like sunshine systems, they also assume that, left to their own devices, contributors and politicians will use money to their advantage in elections and policymaking. While acknowledging the positive impact of reporting and disclosure, proponents of stick systems assume that specific legal restrictions on who can give and how much they can give are necessary to reduce to acceptable levels the advantage that money gives to contributors and politicians in elections and policymaking. Only six states, including Illinois, have *not* adopted some type of stick requirements and mechanisms to augment their sunshine laws.

Systems that try to limit the influence of money on elections and policymaking by substituting public financing linked to voluntary spending limits are carrot systems. Proponents of carrot systems assume that the only way to completely blunt the advantage that money gives to contributors and politicians is to substitute, as much as it is politically possible, "uninterested" public money for "interested" private money and then to tie the receipt of that public money to spending limit agreements.

Neither the federal system nor any of the state systems that have some element of public financing is a pure carrot system. Rather, all are some combination of the carrot and the stick. The federal system is a carrot-and-stick system for presidential elections. The carrot is public financing, while the stick is both contribution limits and voluntary spending limits. Federal legislative elections are stick systems with contribution limits. All state systems with some degree of public financing have carrot-and-stick systems. In 1996, 12 states provided public money for gubernatorial elections, while only three provided public financing for both gubernatorial and legislative

25

elections (Malbin and Gais 1998).

The Illinois campaign finance system is a pure sunshine system. Except for laws, since repealed, to limit contributions from two regulated industries, insurance and horse racing, Illinois has never tried to limit who can give money or how much they can give. No public financing law has ever been signed into law in Illinois.

Campaign Finance Regulation Options for Illinois

States have no obligation to adopt campaign finance regulations that mirror the federal system. But they are bound by the constitutional framework established by *Buckley* and subsequent decisions. In light of these United States Supreme Court decisions, it seems clear that states can require candidates to report the amount and sources of campaign contributions. They can require candidates to account for campaign expenditures. This is the essence of the law in Illinois.

Illinois could pass a law that limits the amount of money that individuals, groups, and corporate entities can contribute to state campaigns. The federal limit is $1,000 per election for individuals and $5,000 for political action committees. But Illinois law places no limit on the amount that an individual or entity can contribute to a political candidate or party.

Illinois also could pass a law that prohibits certain groups (such as labor unions or corporations) or certain categories of groups (e.g., regulated industries, such as public utilities or casino gambling) from contributing to state campaigns or from making independent expenditures. Federal law and most state laws ban unions and corporations from making contributions to candidates directly out of the union's or the corporation's general treasury. Such laws do allow the owners and employees of corporations and the members of unions to form groups (PACs) that can contribute to candidates. But Illinois law places no restrictions on who can contribute to a political candidate or party.

Federal law and most state laws limit the amount that political party committees or candidate political committees can contribute to or spend directly on behalf of a candidate or in coordination with a candidate. But Illinois law places no limit on the amount that can be transferred from a political candidate or party to another political candidate or party.

In the federal system, with its contribution limits, political parties need to make the distinction between hard money contributions, which fall under the limits, and soft money contributions which do not. If Illinois were to adopt contribution limits, it would have to address such questions as whether contributions to political parties could be outside contribution limits (soft money), whether expenditures were independent and therefore outside limits, or coordinated and subject to counting toward limits. But under the wide-open Illinois system, contributions and expenditures are just money.

Illinois could provide for public funding and make acceptance of voluntary spending limits a condition for receiving public funds, as is the case at the federal level for presidential elections. Prior to 1996, only three states had comprehensive systems of public financing which covered both statewide and legislative elections. Since 1996, Maine, Vermont, Massachusetts, and Arizona all adopted comprehensive public financing systems (Dreyfuss 1999). The success of these "clean money" campaigns may signal a willingness of the public to reconsider the idea of the public financing of campaigns.

While Illinois could limit who contributes to a candidate or how much they contribute, Illinois cannot limit how much a candidate spends on an election. Nor can state law limit how much a political party, group, or individual spends independently on behalf of a candidate. But the law can require the reporting and disclosure of the sources and expenditures involved in independent expenditures.

Finally, Illinois is prohibited from limiting expenditures on issue advocacy or "issue ads" by individuals, unions, corporations, or political parties as long as those ads do not expressly advocate the election of a candidate by using specific words such as "vote for," "vote against," "support," or "defeat." It is an open question whether or not Illinois can require the groups or individuals sponsoring them to disclose the amount and the sources of their funds or the amounts and recipients of their expenditures. Issue ads have not been abused in Illinois state elections, but a group or individual might be able to use them to engage in the election process while avoiding Illinois reporting and disclosure requirements.

Illinois' Campaign Finance Law

The state law regulating campaign finance in Illinois is the Illinois Campaign Disclosure Act passed in 1974. It applies to candidates for public office and groups and individuals who support or oppose candidates for public office or support or oppose questions of public policy. Candidate or group receipts and expenditures must exceed certain dollar thresholds in order to be subject to this law. The law requires candidates and groups to keep records of their receipts and expenditures and to file reports at regularly specified intervals.

Beginning with the reporting period of July 1, 1999, to December 31, 1999, committees with receipts or contributions above a certain dollar threshold had to file all reports electronically with the State Board of Elections. Disclosure reports relating to campaigns for local public offices or local referendum questions within a single county are filed with the county clerk and the State Board of Elections. Disclosure reports relating to candidates for statewide office or the state legislature or campaigns for statewide ballot questions are filed with the State Board of Elections.

The board or county clerk receives the disclosure reports and makes them available for public inspection. Since January 1, 2000, the board has been required to make all disclosure reports available on the Internet in a searchable database. The State Board of Elections also has the power to investigate complaints and to assess civil penalties for willful violations of the disclosure law. Those who willfully violate the disclosure law may also be subject to the criminal penalties provided by the law.

The following pages will give more details about Illinois' campaign finance law. Specifically, they examine:
- The general scope and application of state campaign finance rules
- The requirements concerning who must file disclosure reports

- The deadline for filing the reports
- The contents of campaign disclosure reports

The General Scope and Application
of Illinois' Campaign Finance Law

The Illinois State Supreme Court addressed the question of the general intent and applicability of the Illinois Campaign Disclosure Act in a case brought by former Governor Daniel Walker (*Walker v. State Board of Elections*, 391 N.E.2nd 507 (1979)). He challenged a State Board of Elections' finding that a committee formed to pay off campaign debts from his 1972 gubernatorial campaign was required to report its receipts and expenditures to the board. In ruling in favor of the State Board of Elections' position, the court held that:

> The Act is designed to preserve the integrity of the electoral process by requiring full public disclosure of the sources and amounts of campaign contributions and expenditures and the regulation of practices incidental to political campaigns. The legislature wished the public to be informed of the total contributions received and expended by a political committee, the names of significant contributors and of individuals to whom a political committee is indebted.

Who Must File Campaign Disclosure Reports in Illinois?

The Illinois Campaign Disclosure Act provides that:
- Every candidate for public office who accepts contributions or makes expenditures in an aggregate amount exceeding $3,000 in a 12-month period must form a political committee and file a statement of organization and campaign disclosure reports.
- Every individual, trust, partnership, committee, association, corporation, or any organization or group of persons who accepts contributions or makes expenditures during any 12-month period in an aggregate amount exceeding $3,000 on behalf of, or in opposition to, a candidate for public office must form a political committee and file a statement of organization and campaign disclosure reports.

29

- Every individual, trust, partnership, committee, association, corporation, or any organization or group of persons who accepts contributions or makes expenditures during any 12-month period in support of, or opposition to, any question of public policy to be submitted to the electors of an area encompassing no more than one county must form a political committee and file a statement of organization and campaign disclosure reports. For questions of public policy to be submitted to the electors, the dollar threshold is $3,000.

The act also provides that political committees that operate with respect to elections within a single county are designated local political committees. They must file their organization statements and disclosure reports with the county clerk and the State Board of Elections. Political committees that operate with respect to legislative, statewide, and multicounty judicial elections are designated as state political committees. They must file their organization statements and disclosure reports with the State Board of Elections. Political committees that operate as both state and local political committees file their organization statement and disclosure reports with the State Board of Elections and the appropriate county clerk.

What this means is that candidates for local public offices (county board, county officer, school board, mayor, alderman, park board, etc.) and local political party groups must form political committees if their campaign receives or spends more than $3,000 in a 12-month period. The officers of the political committee must file reports of receipts and expenditures with the county clerk of the county in which they are seeking office. A local group formed to support or oppose a policy question being voted on in a local election, such as a referendum on a tax increase for a school district, is required to form a political committee if the group receives or spends more than $3,000 in a campaign to influence the outcome of the vote on that policy question. The officers of that committee must file reports of receipts and expenditures with the county clerk of the county in which the election is being held.

Candidates for statewide office, the state legislature, and judicial offices as well as state and legislative political party groups must form a political committee if their campaign receives or spends more than $3,000 in a 12-month period. The officers of the political committee must file reports of receipts and expenditures with the State Board of Elections. A group formed to support or oppose a question of public policy to be decided by the voters of the state, such as a constitutional amendment, must form a political committee if they receive or spend more than $3,000 in a 12-month period. The officers of that political committee must file reports of receipts and expenditures with the State Board of Elections.

The application of the law to individuals who are not candidates and to groups (other than political party groups) that contribute to candidates or spend resources on behalf of candidates is ambiguous. Administrative rules adopted by the State Board of Elections provide that individuals or corporate entities or labor unions who contribute to a candidate solely from their personal income, membership dues, or profits do not automatically qualify as political action committees regardless of the amount they contribute or spend on behalf of a candidate. Neither an individual who gives $25,000 to a candidate nor a corporation or labor union that gives $25,000 to that candidate's opponent is required to organize as a political committee and file disclosure reports with the State Board of Elections. These contributions would be reported by the candidates receiving them.

State and local political parties and campaign committees formed by legislative chamber groups all organize as political committees and file disclosure reports with the State Board of Elections. It appears that all statewide professional associations that contribute to candidates for local and state office (e.g., the Illinois Realtors Association, the Illinois State Bar Association, the Illinois Hospital and HealthSystems Association (IHHA), etc.) organize political committees and file disclosure reports with the State Board of Elections. The same is true for such employee-based political action committees of corporations as Illinois Power or Central Illinois Public Service, state and regional trade union associations, and statewide public employee unions. Groups formed to influence the outcome of a statewide policy election also organize as political committees and file disclosure reports. Many of the local, regional, and statewide branches of national trade unions organize as political committees and file disclosure reports with the State Board of Elections, but some do not. The same is true for voluntary associations formed to promote political or ideological causes. Some corporations that contribute to candidates for public office in Illinois organize political committees and file disclosure reports with the State Board of Elections, but most do not. The same is true for national voluntary associations, such as the National Rifle Association, which contribute to candidates running for state or local office in Illinois: some file, but most do not.

Faced with scarce resources, the State Board of Elections has chosen to focus on ensuring that candidates and political party groups comply with the disclosure provisions of the law. While the reporting status of noncandidate groups and individuals could be made more consistent by a change in the law (or in the board's interpretation of the law), any contributions that are made by nonfiling groups and corporations can be extrapolated by the public because those contributions should be reported by the candidates who receive them. Still, requiring that all corporations, associations, and groups that contribute to candidates or spend resources on their behalf to organize political committees and file disclosure reports would make it easier for the public to know the relationships that exist between candidates and their financial supporters. The requirements would also increase the public's understanding of the process. In addition, it would help researchers who want to understand campaign finance from a perspective other than that of individual candidates.

When Must Campaign Disclosure Reports Be Filed in Illinois?

The main vehicle for filing Illinois campaign finance disclosure statements is a form called D-2, which is used for filing semi-annual reports as well as for filing pre-election reports. The A-1 form is used for reporting last-minute campaign contributions.

As noted in Table 2.1, the D-2 form may be supported by various schedules. But, at this point it is best to concentrate on the due dates for the D-2 form.

TABLE 2.1

Illinois Campaign Finance Disclosure Reports at a Glance

FORM	WHAT IT COVERS	WHEN IT IS DUE
D-1	Identifies the committee; provides information on its initial funding; outlines the scope of the committee's activity; discloses the committee's political party affiliation (if any).	Ten days from date of creation or five days within 30 days prior to an election.
D-2 (semi-annual)	A semi-annual report that shows income and expenses of the committee.	July 31: for reports covering the period of January 1 to June 30 and January 31: for reports covering the period of July 1 to December 31 for the previous year.
D-2 (pre-election)	A pre-election report that shows income and expenses of the committee; the report is complete as of the 30th day preceding the election.	Not less than 15 days prior to an election.
Schedule A	A schedule that supports the D-2; lists the names and addresses of contributors giving more than $150; also lists information about transfers from other political committees and loans received.	Filed with the D-2
Schedule A-1	Lists the names and addresses of all who contributed $500 or more whose contributions were received in the period 30 days prior to an election.	Filed within two days of receiving a contribution of over $500 in the period 30 days prior to an election.
Schedule B	A schedule that supports the D-2; lists the vendor names, addresses, and amounts of all payments over $150 that the committee made.	Filed with the D-2
Schedule C	A schedule that supports the D-2; shows the activity of debts and obligations in excess of $150.	Filed with the semi-annual D-2
Schedule I	A schedule that supports the D-2; itemizes in-kind contributions valued in excess of $150.	Filed with the D-2

NOTE: This table refers to forms required of political committees that must file disclosure statements with the Illinois State Board of Elections. Only committees that receive or spend $3,000 on behalf of or against candidates running for statewide office or the legislature must file reports with the board. Political committees for noncandidate ballot issues that receive or spend $3,000 also file disclosure reports with the state board. Local political committees file reports with the county clerk and the State Board of Elections.

All political committees must file pre-election reports of campaign contributions on D-2 forms no later than 15 days preceding each election (including primary elections) in which the committee has or is accepting contributions or has or is making expenditures. Such reports shall be complete as of the thirtieth day preceding the election. Any contribution of $500 or more received by the committee between the last date covered in their pre-election campaign report and the date of the election shall be reported within two business days after its receipt on a form called an A-1. (In 1998 the requirements for filing A-1 reports were tightened and the penalties for failing to file these reports were substantially increased.) The intention of requiring pre-election reports and reporting large contributions received during the last month of the campaign is to provide information to the voters when it is most useful: prior to the election.

In addition to any necessary pre-election reports, all political committees that receive or spend $3,000 must file two semi-annual reports of campaign contributions and expenditures on D-2 forms each calendar year. A report covering the period of January 1 to June 30 shall be filed no later than July 31, and a report covering the period of July 1 to December 31 shall be filed no later than January 31 of the following year. These semi-annual reports are recent developments. The law used to require only annual reports at the end of June. This shift to a semi-annual reporting system, starting with the July 1, 1990, to December 31, 1990, period, is one of the few substantive changes made in Illinois' campaign finance disclosure requirements since the law was enacted in 1974. The intention was to provide a more timely accounting of the receipts and expenditures of candidates. The semi-annual system also provides reports that follow the election cycle, particularly in the even-numbered years when a statewide primary takes place in the first six months of the year and a general election occurs during the last six months of the year.

What Must Illinois Campaign Finance Disclosure Reports Contain?

The report of campaign contributions filed by political committees prior to each election and at the end of each six-month reporting period must contain aggregate information for the reporting period on the beginning balance of the committee, the total amount of funds from contributions, transfers to and from other political committees, loans received or made, the total amount of in-kind contributions of goods and services received by the committee, and the total sum of all receipts by the committee for the reporting period. All donations, transfers, loans, and in-kind contributions from a single source that have a value greater than $150 received in the reporting period must be individually itemized. (These itemizations are listed on the schedules that support the D-2 form; see Table 2.1.) Subtotals for itemized and non-itemized contributions, in-kind contributions, loans, and transfers to the committee must also be reported on the D-2.

In addition, the D-2 reports must also contain expenditure information in aggregate and itemized form. All expenditures to a single recipient that exceed $150 in the aggregate for the reporting period and all expenditures made on behalf of a candidate or with regard to a public policy issue that exceed $150 must be itemized. The ending balance reflects the beginning balance, total receipts and total expenditures, but not outstanding debts or expenditures made by other political committees on behalf of the candidate. (Debts are shown on schedule C, and in-kind contributions are shown separately on schedule I.)

Itemized reports of receipts over $150 must list the aggregate contribution amount and the name and mailing address of the source of the receipt. In 1998, the General Assembly adopted a change to require that reports of contributions from individuals over $500 include occupation and employer information. That provision took effect January 1, 1999. This requirement at the $200 level has been part of the federal system since 1974. Itemized reports of expenditures over $150 must list the recipient of the expenditure, the amount of the receipt or expenditure, the date it was made, and the aggregate total to the recipient for the reporting period.

Why Is Illinois So Different?

Some of those opposed to reforming the federal campaign finance system offer the idea of deregulating the federal system. (To their credit, most deregulators favor putting in place an electronic reporting and disclosure system.)

But what could happen to federal elections with an unregulated system? No one has to wonder. They only need to look to Illinois, with its quarter-century history of completely wide-open campaign funding practices. Given the diversity of the state and the competitiveness of its elections, political scientists often argue that Illinois is a microcosm of the nation. As such, it is likely that the same patterns of election competition, interest group activity, and legislative leadership and executive power that have developed in Illinois would develop at the national level under a completely deregulated system. Because Illinois' system of electronic filing and Internet-based disclosure is so new, it is impossible to know what effect a true level of sunshine exposure would have on the patterns of competition and influence that have developed under a completely deregulated system.

Let's go back to the discussion of carrots, sticks, and sunshine for some perspective. In a 1996 survey of state campaign finance systems, Michael Malbin and Thomas Gais found basic sunshine systems in only 12 states. Of these, only Texas combines big-money politics with a wide-open system in a way that compares with Illinois. Candidates running for public office in the large majority of states compete in stick systems with contribution limits and prohibitions on direct contributions from corporations and unions. Only a small number of governors and a small group of legislative candidates compete in systems that also provide some form of public finance in a carrot-and-stick approach.

Why is Illinois a state so far from the norm? Proponents of sunshine systems often contend that contributing and spending money is a form of political speech protected by the First Amendment. In defending the free-speech rights of all citizens, they firmly believe that any restrictions are constitutionally suspect. As such, the only way to regulate the impact of money on politics is to provide complete disclosure, which, it is assumed, will lead to self-regulation for either ethical or political reasons because everyone will know who is taking money from whom. Thus, contributors and politicians will modify their behavior to avoid personal or political scandal.

Illinois' campaign finance system was not born out of any concern for First Amendment free-speech rights. Nor was it adopted as an antidote for chaos and imperfections born of the overregulation of a stick approach. Rather, Illinois' campaign finance system reflects and nurtures the dominant individualistic political culture of the state. The free flow of money allows the players to maximize their financial resources and pursue power and advantage without regard to limits or legal distinctions. A free market approach to campaign finance is completely consistent with the market-oriented approach to politics and public policy that is the hallmark of Illinois politics.

The legislative leaders and governors who have controlled Illinois politics since the 1970s have largely been products or willing converts to Illinois political culture. In the last third of the twentieth century, the power of the legislative leaders and the governor grew to a level unprecedented in Illinois politics. The 1970 Illinois Constitution did not provide an initiative process through which citizens could pass petitions and put a binding question of public policy on the ballot to be decided by a popular vote. Only a limited initiative process dealing with matters of legislative structure and procedure was allowed. Ultimately, it is those who benefit most from the campaign finance system who will have to take the initiative to change it. Given the dynamics of Illinois' political culture and the personal histories of the governor and the legislative leaders in power at the turn of the new century, it would be surprising if Illinois soon has any system of campaign finance other than the one that has existed since 1974.

Draining the Ethical Swamp

In general, the power relationships that shaped and are maintained by Illinois' campaign finance system were strengthened in the final quarter of the twentieth century. But, it is true that the ethics of raising and spending money did undergo significant modifications in the late 1990s.

The most dramatic change was in the area of the personal use of campaign funds. On January 1, 1999, it became illegal for candidates

or elected officials to use money raised through a political committee for personal benefit. Until that change, candidates and public
officials could — and did — use money raised from campaign contributions to buy houses, clothes, cars, and season tickets to professional sports events. They could — and did — give themselves no-
interest loans and pay themselves stipends in addition to their public salary. Most of these actions required that they declare the campaign money as personal income and pay state and federal income
tax. But the only limits were moral. And, to be fair, *most* candidates
and public officials did not take advantage of the absence of legal
restrictions. However, the few who did abuse the system became
symbols of the excesses of Illinois' wide-open campaign finance system. Given the increasing drumbeat of public and media criticism,
the campaign finance bill passed in 1998 included a ban on the personal use of campaign funds. However, in typical Illinois fashion, all
existing public officials were covered by a grandfather clause that
allows them to make personal-use expenditures out of campaign
funds equal to the amount each had in his or her fund on June 30,
1998. In the case of George Ryan, who was elected governor in
November 1998, that clause is worth more than $4.8 million.

The bill that stopped personal use of campaign funds also prohibits soliciting or receiving campaign contributions on state property, prohibits the holding of fundraising events in Springfield on
days the legislature is in session, and bans certain gifts from lobbyists to elected officials and public employees. All of these changes
were rooted in political scandals that have become symbols for the
excesses and moral blindness of the current system.

State employees selling fundraising tickets at work during lunch
hours and breaks had long been an integral part of Illinois' patronage system. It also was the source of periodic public embarrassment,
when some state employees violated the letter, as well as the spirit,
of the long-standing legal prohibition on doing political work on
state time. Added to this was the image captured in press accounts
of former legislator turned lobbyist Al Ronan handing out
envelopes containing campaign contributions to legislators as they
left the House chamber one day during the 1993 fall legislative ses-

sion (Fitzgerald 1994). During the 1990s, holding fundraisers in Springfield during the legislative session became increasingly popular. With all the major lobbyists in town for the session, an evening or morning event was an efficient, cost-effective way of raising money. However, the closeness of the fundraising and policymaking activities raised questions of pressure and appearance. In the words of one long-time player who represented a public agency, "If a committee chairman is going to hold a fundraiser the morning of the deadline for bills to be out of committee, he might as well just hold an auction on the Statehouse lawn." Finally, the Management Services of Illinois (MSI) scandal of 1997 hinged on bribes of food and trips as well as cash payments made by a private sector company with a lucrative state contract to employees of the state agency administering that contract. The scandal publicly raised the question of where the line between gifts and bribes was drawn. All of these events put a public face on the need for campaign contribution and spending restrictions, and the fallout from these events provided the momentum for change.

It should be noted, however, that one of the primary exemptions from the 1998 gift ban was for "food and beverages consumed on the premises." As a practical matter, this allows lobbyists to continue the long-standing tradition of wining and dining legislators. Under a law that took effect January 1, 1999, it is illegal for a lobbyist to buy a bottle of wine and a frozen lobster and give them to a legislator, but it is still legal for a lobbyist to take a legislator to dinner and buy him or her a lobster dinner and an expensive bottle of wine.

At one level, the changes of the late 1990s merely introduce common sense provisions that bring the personal ethical level of the Illinois campaign finance system up from the bottom of the barrel to a level that's at least comparable to the campaign ethics of other states. But given the preceding quarter century of inaction, it is remarkable that these changes made it to the House and Senate floors, let alone got passed and signed into law. In fact, outside influences were at work. The reform measures of the late 1990s were the direct result of a dialogue between representatives of the four legislative leaders and Governor Jim Edgar, but that dialogue was precipitated through the efforts of former U.S. Senator Paul Simon and Governor Edgar's former press secretary, Mike Lawrence. The purpose was to explore whether any common ground existed on proposed changes to the campaign finance law that could be put into a bipartisan bill that the four leaders and the governor would sign off on. The resulting process and the successful passage of a bill at the end of the 1998 session is a tribute to the leadership and hard work of Lawrence and Simon. It also shows that such provisions as the personal-use ban are impossible to vote against, once they make it to a vote. It is getting such changes to the floor for a vote that usually is impossible. Left to its own devices, the legislature often plays games with these types of reform measures. One chamber will pass the measure, only if it knows the other is sure to reject it. Or, a more complicated shell game arises when the chambers pass two different reform measures and then fail to come to consensus on a single measure. (This is a brilliant ploy because a majority of politicians can then claim they voted for a reform measure, without the painful reform actually having to occur.) In 1998, improving the ethical face of Illinois' campaign finance system may have been the right thing to do, but it passed because it was on the floor, and it was on the floor because those who controlled the political system were persuaded that it was good politics to support it. (Or maybe they were persuaded that it was bad politics to oppose it.) While the presence of Simon and Lawrence made this an unusual process, their success suggests that strategies and mechanisms for change are possible, even in Illinois.

Making Sunshine Work:
Electronic Filing and Internet Access

In the case of *Walker v. State Board of Elections*, the Illinois Supreme Court held that information about campaign contributions and expenditures should be disclosed and reported because "the legislature wished the public to be informed" about how much was being spent on political campaigns and who was financing them. While the Illinois Campaign Disclosure Act has been successful in compelling a more detailed record of campaign contributions and expenditures, the wish that the public be informed has gone largely unfulfilled, until recently.

From the mid-1970s and throughout the 1980s and 1990s, campaign disclosure reports from political committees across the state flowed into the offices of the State Board of Elections prior to every election and twice a year during January and July. The staff of the board copied those reports onto microfiche and stored them away. For most of the general public, that was the end of story. Except for frequent inspections by the opponents of the candidates filing the reports, occasional inspections by newspaper, radio, and television reporters, and infrequent inspections by academic researchers, the mountain of data on file at the State Board of Elections went undisturbed year after year.

Part of the reason for the lack of campaign finance information available to the general public was financial. While creation of a State Board of Elections is mandated by the 1970 Illinois Constitution, it has shared the same financial history as most state campaign watchdog/disclosure agencies. As one observer noted in a 1992 article in *Governing* magazine: "They are treated like poor stepchildren. They rarely have the staff or resources to analyze what is happening to the campaign finance system as a whole, to perform specific audits of candidates' returns or even to make the data available in a form that allows people to figure out, say, how much the dairy industry has contributed to a particular candidate" (Gurwitt 1992).

The Illinois State Board of Elections' budget has been slow to grow, even in good fiscal times. The major budget cut suffered by the board in fiscal year 1992 was only the most recent hit the board has absorbed in bad fiscal times. A lack of staff and a lack of equipment and contractual money have severely limited the computerization of the board's record keeping and retrieval activities. Not having even aggregate information on a database prior to 1990 has made it very difficult for the board's staff to prepare even basic reports on campaign contribution and expenditure activity. The 1992 report on aggregate receipts and expenditures by candidates for statewide office and for seats in the legislature for the 1990 election was the first such general report issued by the board in its history.

The lack of resources provided by the governor and legislature through the appropriation process is ultimately a reflection of the primary reason why information about campaign finance in Illinois is so hard to obtain. Simply put, Illinois historically has been operating under a political climate that discouraged public dissemination of campaign finance information. Back in 1974, state Senator John Nimrod, a Skokie Republican, offered an amendment to the proposed new state campaign disclosure law to eliminate the authority of the State Board of Elections to prepare and publish reports on the information contained in the disclosure reports. In arguing he said, "I'm sure that we do not want to prohibit or restrict any of this information from reaching the persons who are interested in getting it, but it certainly is not a responsibility of [the legislature to pay] to publish this information." His amendment failed, but the general lack of enthusiasm for disclosing and reporting campaign finance information displayed in the floor debates over the 1974 law also extended to the question of disseminating the information. Those attitudes are still dominant within the Illinois political community, but there are signs that the political culture in Illinois is starting to change.

In 1995, the State Board of Elections created a database of contributions to candidates for legislative and statewide office for the 1994 general election. That database was subsequently made available to the public. For the first time, comprehensive information about who was funding Illinois campaigns was available. The board continued to produce databases for each subsequent six-month period up to and including the 1998 general election.

While this level of information was light-years ahead of anything previously available, there were two serious drawbacks. First, it was very expensive and time consuming to do the data entry. The delay meant that comprehensive information about an election was not available until four to six months after it occurred. More important, no information on expenditures was available.

Changes in the law in 1997 now mandate that the State Board of Elections provide access to information about both receipts and expenditures to the public in a database posted on an Internet web site. When the law first took effect, electronic filing of reports was allowed, but not required. So, the board was faced with the task of taking hard-copy reports generated from electronic databases maintained by political committees and entering those records into a database to be accessed electronically by the public. This was technology in reverse. The 1998 changes in the campaign finance disclosure law require political committees that exceed a $25,000 threshold of receipts or expenditures to file electronically. Implementing mandatory electronic filing did not take place without problems. The board delayed the starting date from the reporting period for the first half of 1999 to the second half of 1999. With no resources to produce even a receipt database for the first half of 1999, there is a six-month gap in the electronic record. To exacerbate the situation, bills were introduced in fall 1999 to make electronic filing voluntary rather than mandatory. (How much of that was prompted by a resistance to new technology and how much was due to a growing realization of the potential power of the public's having ready access to campaign finance information is hard to say.) But a funny thing happened in Illinois. The drive to make electronic filing voluntary failed. The law remained unchanged. Not only do we have mandatory electronic filing, but the dollar threshold that mandates electronic filing will drop to $10,000 on July 1, 2003.

With the filing of the first set of reports on January 31, 2000, Illinois moved into a new era. Citizens, the news media, pubic interest groups, and other politicians now have easy access to the campaign finance records of local, county, judicial, legislative, and statewide elected officials. Illinois now has what is considered by many to be the best electronic filing and disclosure process in the country.

Like many of the changes in society that are driven by technology, there are alternative futures for the way this information will influence the political process in Illinois. As good as the new system is, only a limited amount of current information is available before an election or before roll-call votes in the legislature. The comprehensive reports of receipts and expenditures for the previous six months are still filed at the end of January and July, a full two to three months after the time when their sunshine effect would be the greatest. The potential exists to use electronic disclosure to radically change the dynamics of political campaigns and legislative policy debates by making information available on a real-time basis. Realizing that potential will be one of the themes of the concluding chapter.

Funding
Illinois Politics

Private and
Political Money

Funding Illinois Politics

The price of politics in Illinois keeps going up. During the election cycle of 1997-1998, legislative and statewide candidates and officeholders and the two state political parties raised a record $107.8 million[1] and spent a record $91 million. The old records of $88 million in contributions and $74 million in expenditures were set in the 1993-1994 election cycle, another gubernatorial election year. The winning candidate for governor in 1998, George Ryan, raised a record $16.1 million. That same year, the spending in two state Senate races topped the $1 million mark, and spending in two state House legislative races exceeded $800,000.

The largest source of the money that flows into Illinois politics is the private economic sector: corporations, trade associations, unions, and professional associations. In the 1990s, money from those sources averaged slightly more than 55 percent of all the money contributed. The next largest source of funding for Illinois politics is the political sector. Money and services given by one political committee to another account for an average of 20 percent of all money contributed. The next largest source of funding is contributions from individuals as individuals (not as surrogates for private economic interests or political interests). Contributions from individuals account for an average of 15 percent of the money in Illinois politics. Finally, an average of 10 percent of the money contributed comes in the form of not-itemized contributions. Under Illinois law, contributions of less than $150 do not have to be individually itemized. Instead, they can be reported in a lump sum. These small contributions may be from individuals, but they also may be from private economic interests or political committees. There is no way to tell.

The breakdown from the 1997-1998 election cycle represented in

[1]All dollar figures, unless otherwise noted, were generated from an Illinois campaign finance database created by the author. Support for the database was provided by The Joyce Foundation and the Institute for Public Affairs at the University of Illinois at Springfield. The database contains receipt and expenditure records beginning with January 1, 1993, and is updated every six months. As of August 2000, the database contained more than 400,000 records from more than 600 candidates for legislative and statewide offices.

Figure 3.1 shows, in total, where contributions to legislative and statewide candidates and officeholders and state political parties in Illinois came from for that two-year election period. Contributions from private economic sector sources totaled $52.4 million, while political sources accounted for $21.2 million. Individuals gave $16.6 million, and small contributors gave $12.4 million. Interest income, loans, refunds, and unclassified contributions generated an additional $5.2 million for candidates. In order to understand the role of money in Illinois politics, it is necessary to examine the sources of both private and political money and the relationships they create.

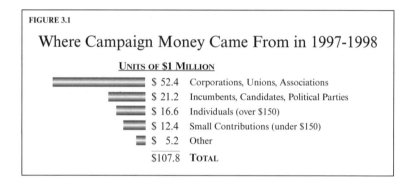

FIGURE 3.1

Where Campaign Money Came From in 1997-1998

UNITS OF $1 MILLION

	$ 52.4	Corporations, Unions, Associations
	$ 21.2	Incumbents, Candidates, Political Parties
	$ 16.6	Individuals (over $150)
	$ 12.4	Small Contributions (under $150)
	$ 5.2	Other
	$107.8	TOTAL

Political Money from Private Sources

Private sector money comes into the Illinois campaign finance system from three main sources. First are the private economic sector sources. As discussed above, these are unions, corporations, trade associations, and large single-issue interest groups. Second are individuals who make large contributions. Third are individuals, groups, and corporations that make small political contributions. Each of these private sector interests has its motives for contributing money, and some of the larger contributors have distinct contribution strategies, which will be examined in the following pages.

Private Economic Sector Money

The greatest portion of private economic sector money comes from business interests, either individual corporations, such as Ameritech or Commonwealth Edison, or trade associations, such as the Illinois Hospital and HealthSystems Association or the Illinois Manufacturers' Association. On average, these business interests account for more than 60 percent of the private economic sector dollars donated during a two-year election cycle. Typically, labor interests (trade and public sector unions) contribute between 15 and 20 percent of the private economic sector dollars donated during a two-year election cycle, and professional associations (such as the Illinois State Medical Society or the Illinois Association of Realtors) match those contributions, kicking in between 15 and 20 percent of the private economic sector donations. The remaining 3 to 6 percent comes from lobbyists, ideological coalitions, and single-issue groups. The breakdown from the 1997-1998 election cycle, as shown in Figure 3.2, is typical. In that election cycle, business interests contributed $32.3 million, professional interests contributed $10.9 million, labor interests $9.2 million, and the remaining $5.2 million came from lobbyists and ideological or single-interest groups.

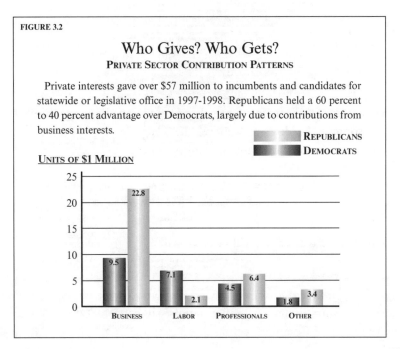

FIGURE 3.2

Who Gives? Who Gets?
PRIVATE SECTOR CONTRIBUTION PATTERNS

Private interests gave over $57 million to incumbents and candidates for statewide or legislative office in 1997-1998. Republicans held a 60 percent to 40 percent advantage over Democrats, largely due to contributions from business interests.

REPUBLICANS
DEMOCRATS

UNITS OF $1 MILLION

BUSINESS 9.5 / 22.8
LABOR 7.1 / 2.1
PROFESSIONALS 4.5 / 6.4
OTHER 1.8 / 3.4

Within the broad private economic sector categories of business, labor, professional, and other, the three biggest contributor groups are lawyers and law firms, trade unions, and manufacturing companies and their associations. In the 1997-1998 election cycle, manufacturing interests alone gave more than $4.9 million to legislative and statewide candidates and elected officials. Figure 3.3 presents a detailed breakdown of the contributions of these groups for that election cycle. The distribution is typical for private economic sector contributor groups during a two-year period.

FIGURE 3.3

Contributions by Industry or Group

More money is contributed to Illinois politicians by law firms, trade unions, and manufacturing companies than any other groups or industries. Not all of the contributors from an industry or group have the same interests and concerns, but the following list is an indication of the relative strength of groups and industries as contributors in 1997-1998.

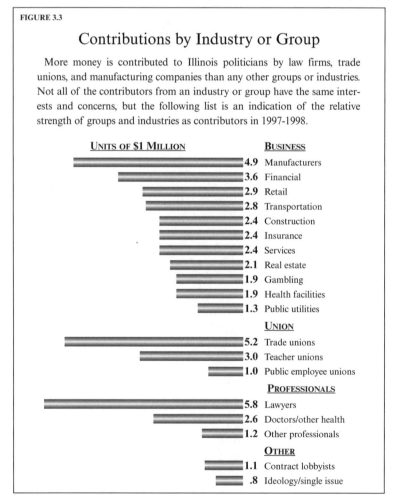

UNITS OF $1 MILLION	BUSINESS
4.9	Manufacturers
3.6	Financial
2.9	Retail
2.8	Transportation
2.4	Construction
2.4	Insurance
2.4	Services
2.1	Real estate
1.9	Gambling
1.9	Health facilities
1.3	Public utilities
	UNION
5.2	Trade unions
3.0	Teacher unions
1.0	Public employee unions
	PROFESSIONALS
5.8	Lawyers
2.6	Doctors/other health
1.2	Other professionals
	OTHER
1.1	Contract lobbyists
.8	Ideology/single issue

The range of economic interests in Illinois represented in Figure 3.3 clearly shows tremendous diversity. Almost every conceivable private sector concern — business, labor, and professional — appears to be using campaign contributions as an essential part of its efforts to elect candidates or influence public policy. With no contribution limits and no prohibition on contributions from corporations, both organized interests and individual corporate entities can and do bring their substantial financial resources to bear on the process.

The identity of the largest individual private sector contributors also provides insight into the basic nature of the political system in Illinois. The top 20 contributors to legislative and statewide candidates and officeholders and the two state political parties for the 1997-1998 election cycle are listed in Figure 3.4.

FIGURE 3.4

Interest Groups with Cash Clout

If your interest group had given $25,000 to Illinois politicians, it would be in 337th place on a list of 1997-1998 contributors. Giving $100,000 would have put your group into the top 100, at number 94. Breaking into the top 10 would have taken almost half a million dollars. Being number one would have cost over $1.9 million.

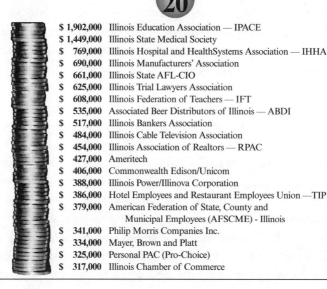

$ 1,902,000	Illinois Education Association — IPACE
$ 1,449,000	Illinois State Medical Society
$ 769,000	Illinois Hospital and HealthSystems Association — IHHA
$ 690,000	Illinois Manufacturers' Association
$ 661,000	Illinois State AFL-CIO
$ 625,000	Illinois Trial Lawyers Association
$ 608,000	Illinois Federation of Teachers — IFT
$ 535,000	Associated Beer Distributors of Illinois — ABDI
$ 517,000	Illinois Bankers Association
$ 484,000	Illinois Cable Television Association
$ 454,000	Illinois Association of Realtors — RPAC
$ 427,000	Ameritech
$ 406,000	Commonwealth Edison/Unicom
$ 388,000	Illinois Power/Illinova Corporation
$ 386,000	Hotel Employees and Restaurant Employees Union —TIP
$ 379,000	American Federation of State, County and Municipal Employees (AFSCME) - Illinois
$ 341,000	Philip Morris Companies Inc.
$ 334,000	Mayer, Brown and Platt
$ 325,000	Personal PAC (Pro-Choice)
$ 317,000	Illinois Chamber of Commerce

From 1988 to 1998, eight groups were habitually among the top 10 biggest contributors. They were the Illinois Education Association, the Illinois State Medical Society, the Illinois Manufacturers' Association, the Illinois Hospital and HealthSystems Association, the Illinois Bankers Association, the Illinois Trial Lawyers Association, the Associated Beer Distributors of Illinois, and the Illinois Association of Realtors. During the 1995-1996 and 1997-1998 election cycles, the Illinois Cable Television Association, the Ameritech Corporation, the Illinois Federation of Teachers, and Philip Morris Companies Inc. also broke into the top ten. The continued presence of these interests among the largest contributors to Illinois politics indicates not only their ability and willingness to use campaign contributions to further their interests, but also an ongoing concern over the impact of Illinois state government on their interests.

For the 1997-1998 election cycle, the largest single contributor to Illinois politics was the Illinois Education Association (IEA) with more than $1.9 million. Next came the Illinois State Medical Society with more than $1.45 million. The IEA and the medical society have long been the "big two" contributors. After leading all contributors in every election cycle in the decade, the Illinois State Medical Society fell to second place in 1997-1998. Seven other groups topped $500,000 in 1997-1998, with the Illinois Hospital and HealthSystems Association coming in third overall with $769,000 in contributions. Ninety-three groups gave more than $100,000, while 336 groups gave at least $25,000. The top 20 private economic sector groups gave more than $11.9 million in 1997-1998, up from approximately $9.3 and $7.7 million the two previous cycles.

With one exception, the types of interests represented by single-issue groups — ideological, environmental, public interest, consumer, mental health, or public health advocates — are absent from Figure 3.4. The one exception is Personal PAC, a pro-choice group that contributes to candidates based on their positions on abortion rights. Some single-interest groups are nonprofit organizations that are prohibited by federal tax law from making campaign contributions. But that's likely not the reason why more issue groups don't crack the list of the top 20 private economic sector donors. The larger reality is that groups of these types have very little money compared to the trade and professional associations and individual corporations that dominate private sector contributions.

In life and in politics, those with money have an advantage over those without money. But it is not the case that *only* groups or entities that contribute exercise influence in Illinois politics. Money is only one of a number of resources that groups can use to advance their issues. For example, groups representing farmers and agriculture interests are not large contributors. This does not mean that the interests of farmers in particular and agriculture in general are not well-represented in the Illinois legislature. They are. While large campaign contributions do not play a key role in their success, agricultural interests benefit from strong organizations and great sympathy among many legislators for the interest of the "family farmer."

That is all well and good. But the fact remains that, compared to other states and the federal system, the Illinois campaign finance system tends to emphasize the money advantage by allowing every interest that wishes to contribute unlimited amounts to candidates and officeholders. How significant that advantage is in elections and in making public policy will be explored in the next two chapters.

WHY DO PRIVATE INTERESTS CONTRIBUTE?

Why did private economic sector interests give more than $57 million to Illinois politicians and political parties in the 1997-1998 election cycle, while individuals contributed more than $16 million and small contributors gave more than $12 million? The specific reasons are probably as numerous as the givers themselves. All private money is "interested" money in the sense that the giver wants something. At a general level, the motives of contributors fall into four basic categories.

1. Contributors want to help their friends.
2. Contributors want to help good people.
3. Contributors want to elect people who help them.
4. Contributors want to help those already in power so those in power will help the contributors.

These are not mutually exclusive categories, although most contributions fall primarily within one of them.

Tom Loftus, former longtime speaker of the Wisconsin State Assembly, says that the essence of running for public office is asking your friends for money and strangers for their vote. In looking for the connection between contributor and politician, it is easy to miss the obvious link: a personal relationship. When the owner of a small retail store contributes to the campaign of a state legislator, the goal may be to advance the agenda of the Illinois Retail Merchants Association or the Illinois Chamber of Commerce. But it is more likely that the connection is personal. The candidate and the merchant may be lodge brothers, or cousins, or tennis partners, or they may have been high school classmates. The candidate's law firm may buy office supplies from the merchant. The candidate may have been the cookie chairman for the merchant's daughter's Girl Scout troop, or the merchant may teach the candidate's Sunday school class. When determining motives for giving, it's probably not wise to assume a personal connection when, for example, a legislative candidate campaigning to represent people in deep southern Illinois receives a contribution from a Chicago labor union or a Rockford-based manufacturing corporation. But friendship or some other personal connection explains a very large number of the contributions made to candidates by individuals. It also accounts for many of the contributions that businesses make to legislative candidates running in the district in which the business is located.

In addition to personal connections, another often underestimated motivation for giving money is a desire to help good people win public office. The cynicism and media scrutiny that pervade public life often lead to the wholesale discounting of or total disregard for any thought that people give money to candidates or elected public officials because they think the person is doing or will do a good job. It does seem safe to assume that when the Illinois Education Association gave more than $235,000 to gubernatorial candidate George Ryan in 1998 that more than a desire for "good government" was involved. Still, it is difficult to come up with a better explanation of U.S. Senator John McCain's success in raising money over the Internet during his presidential primary campaign in the spring of 2000 other than the desire of individuals to promote the campaign of a candidate they felt was a good man or had good ideas. People give money to help good people get elected.

While it is a mistake to assume that all interests are selfish or contrary to the general public welfare, it is also clear that most private money is not contributed for reasons of personal relationships or to promote the general goals of good government. Instead, the goal is either: a) to help elect people to office who will pursue the donor's interests, or b) to help those already in power so they will start (or continue to) pursue the donor's interests.

Often these goals overlap. Depending on the resources and the issues that a labor union, corporation, group, or individual has, either or both goals may be appropriate and lead to specific contribution strategies. In fact, campaign contributions in these circumstances are best understood as part of larger lobbying strategies. Individuals, groups, and entities want to influence legislative or executive policy. Money is a tool, a means to an end.

The beer distributors in Illinois are organized as the Associated Beer Distributors of Illinois. They were a top ten contributor to Illinois elections throughout the 1990s. It turns out that candidates for public office rarely run on pro- or anti-beer platforms. Other than taxes, few "beer" issues come up in the General Assembly. The beer distributors are not fighting other interests for a share of the state budget. Generally, they just want to be left alone. They give money to incumbent legislators, the legislative leaders, and the governor. They almost never contribute to candidates who are challenging incumbents, and they do not directly get involved in campaigns beyond contributing money. Within reason, they really do not care who gets elected to the legislature or elected governor, as long as they can establish a good relationship with those elected officials. They support the "incumbent" party rather than the Democratic or Republican Party. If the Democrats control the legislature, the beer distributors' contributions lean to the Democrats because there are more Democratic members and the Democratic leaders have more power. Should the Republicans gain control of the legislature, the contributions of the beer distributors would shift in favor of the Republicans. This is a strategy of helping those already in power so they will protect the donor's interests. Given the policy environment, a strategy of maintaining good relationships with whomever is in power is an appropriate one for the beer distributors. People give money to help those in power so they will help them.

Illinois public school teachers are represented by two major organizations, the Illinois Education Association (IEA) and the Illinois Federation of Teachers (IFT). (The Chicago Teachers Union is affiliated with the IFT.) Together, these groups gave $2.5 million to legislative and statewide candidates and officeholders in the 1997-1998 election cycle. Teacher unions want increased funding for public education. That goal competes for state funding with all of the other groups and interests that want money from the state budget. Almost every candidate, Democrat and Republican, runs for office on a platform of improving education. However, there are major differences of opinion as to what the public education problems are and which solutions are most appropriate. Teacher unions have a strong interest in influencing the outcome of the policy debate over education reform.

To achieve their policy goals, teacher unions pursue contribution strategies with a dominant electoral focus. The vast majority of their contributions go not to parties but to legislative candidates, with a large portion going to incumbents and challengers in contested races. Both the IEA and the IFT identify candidates who share their policy positions and support increased funding for public education. The teacher unions then contribute heavily to those races and work on them directly by providing in-kind services and campaign volunteers. The goal is to maintain or increase the number of legislators who can be counted on to support the specific goals of the teacher unions. The teacher unions also contribute to legislative leaders and the governor, but electing supporters to the legislature is the core of their contribution strategy. Who gets elected to the legislature is critically important to the teacher unions' being able to further their interests, and union contribution patterns reflect this. People and organizations give money to help elect people who will help them.

Groups and entities with specific policy interests tend to adopt either an electoral focus or an access/influence focus. To some extent, the choice is dictated by the nature of the policy interests involved. As previously noted, these are not mutually exclusive. Many groups and entities combine parts of both. Access-oriented groups, who give to incumbents and usually avoid contested elections, may give larger than normal contributions to an incumbent supporter who is facing a tough re-election battle. And some election-oriented groups will also contribute regularly to friendly incumbents from safe districts who have no opposition for re-election. On balance, it requires a much greater amount of money to be involved effectively in contested elections than to target contributions toward legislative leaders, key incumbent legislators, or the governor. Groups with limited resources may have little choice other than to give to the legislative leaders and a few key incumbents. The largest private sector contributors to Illinois politics have strategic options that are beyond the reach of most other private sector interests.

There is no better example of a group that combines an electoral focus with an access/influence focus than the Illinois State Medical Society. The society gives large contributions to candidates in contested races in the general election. Those candidates are usually Republican. The medical society also makes large contributions to the Republican legislative leaders during the general election period. Overall, its contribution patterns suggest that the medical society would prefer that the Republicans control the legislature. However, the group also gives money to Democratic legislative leaders and to incumbent legislators in safe districts from both parties. In addition, the society will make contributions to candidates in contested primaries from both parties. The fact that the Illinois State Medical Society had $1.45 million to contribute in the 1997-1998 election cycle certainly provided that group with the freedom to pursue multiple strategies. But just having sufficient money does not alone dictate strategy. The IEA made $1.9 million in contributions using a very strong bipartisan electoral focus on individual members. On the other hand, the IFT made $608,000 in contributions using a very strong electoral focus on individual members, but gave almost all of its contributions to Democratic candidates.

CONTRIBUTION STRATEGIES

The reasons groups and individuals make donations often dictate (and are thus often reflected in) their campaign contribution strategies. Contributors who want to help a friend or a candidate they consider a good person get elected make few strategic choices. The only issues are how much to give and perhaps when to give. In contrast, contributors who want to maximize the number of people elected to office who support their issues face a number of strategic choices. The same is true for contributors who want to maximize the influence they have on those already in office. Should they focus their contributions on incumbents or challengers, Democrats or Republicans, legislators or the governor, individual legislators or the legislative leaders? Depending on their goals, their issues, and their resources, contributors tend to adopt one of a small number of broad strategies.

In the 1991-1992 election cycle, the Democrats controlled both chambers of the Illinois General Assembly, just as they had done since 1973. After the 1992 elections, the Republicans took control of the Senate, and, after the 1994 election, the Republicans took control of the House. As a result, the Republicans controlled both chambers during the 1995-1996 election cycle. Looking at the shifts in the partisanship of the contributions of some of the major contributor groups between the 1991-1992 and 1995-1996 election cycles helps reveal the underlying goals of some private economic sector groups and the strategies they used to pursue those goals. The Illinois State Medical Society and the Illinois Manufacturers' Association became much more Republican in their contributions (shifts of 17 and 21 percentage points), while the Illinois Trial Lawyers Association and the state public employee union (AFSCME) became much more Democratic in their contributions (shifts of 10 and 11 percentage points). These groups cared very strongly who controlled the legislature, and the 1996 election was an opportunity to reverse or solidify the change that occurred in 1994. The increased partisanship of their contributions is exactly what would be expected for groups with a partisan electoral focus to their lobbying strategy.

Conversely, the contributions of the realtors' association, beer

58

distributors' association, bankers' association, hospital association, and cable TV association all shifted from a majority going to the Democrats in 1991-1992 to a majority going to the Republicans in 1995-1996. These were dramatic changes, ranging from 17 percentage points for the beer distributors and bankers to 38 percentage points for the cable TV association. These groups use their money to have access to or have influence with legislators. They are interested in building relationships with whomever is in power. With a shift from a Democrat-controlled legislature to one controlled by Republicans, one would expect money to follow power for access- and influence-oriented groups, which is exactly what happened.

ACCESS/INFLUENCE LOBBYING STRATEGIES

As previously noted, the Associated Beer Distributors of Illinois want access and influence with those in power. As a group, they give a large amount of money, ranking eighth in contributions in the 1997-1998 election cycle. While the beer distributors do not have a large membership, their members live throughout the state. The association rarely has a pro-active legislative agenda, and it instead concentrates on keeping what it considers "bad things," like increases in liquor taxes, from happening. While beer is not universally popular, the association does, in some respects, represent a constituency group that has currency with the legislators: "Joe Sixpack." Particularly when opposing increases in liquor prices, the image of trying to stop Springfield from making life a little harder for the working man or woman who just wants to enjoy a beer at the end of a tough week is a very sympathetic lobbying position.

At the core of the beer distributors' strategy is a large number of contributions to incumbent legislators on a bipartisan basis. The group contributes on a regular basis to legislators during both years of the election cycle. Because they are giving to those in power, their contributions will tilt toward whatever party controls the legislature. Their contributions to legislators are in the moderate range, $1,000 to $5,000 each per year. They don't get involved with individual legislative campaigns beyond making contributions of money or goods and services, such as contributing beverages for legislators' fundraising events. The distributors also give to all the Republican and

Democratic legislative leaders in both the House and the Senate. While their focus is legislative, they also make contributions to incumbent governors who are at least neutral to their interests. Overall, their contribution strategy is nonelectoral, member-focused, bipartisan, and status quo-oriented. It is a strategy to help those in power so they will help you.

The contribution strategy of the Illinois CPA Society is quite similar to that of the beer distributors. The accountants' society is generally not interested in influencing who gets elected. It wants access to the leaders and individual members of the legislature. The CPA society does not have a strong interest in the executive branch. It is protectionist and status quo-oriented and with some reason. It is hard to remember the last time a really hot CPA bill came before the Illinois General Assembly. The society contributes on a regular basis to a large number of incumbent legislators. It is generally bipartisan in its giving. The CPAs do differ from the beer distributors in that the CPA society gives a larger portion of its contributions to legislative leaders and that its contributions to individual legislators are more modest.

Other groups that tend toward access/influence, member-focused, bipartisan, status quo-oriented contribution strategies are the Illinois Association of Realtors, the Illinois Bankers Association, the Illinois Cable Television Association, the Illinois Hospital and HealthSystems Association, and the Illinois New Car and Truck Dealers Association. Some may be more partisan and others more leadership-oriented, but all of them tend to focus on building relations with those in power rather than trying to influence the elections that determine who has power.

While some access- and influence-oriented groups and entities that want to maintain the status quo focus on individual members of the General Assembly to provide influence in the process, others focus on the legislative leaders. Philip Morris Companies Inc. is a good example. Philip Morris is not interested in directly influencing who gets elected to the General Assembly. (Few candidates run on a pro-tobacco platform.) And given the negative image of tobacco, putting a lot of tobacco money directly in a competitive legislative race might do more harm than good for the candidate Philip Morris is trying to help. The company wants access and influence with those already holding power. Its strategy is to make large contributions to legislative leaders on a nonpartisan basis. Philip Morris also makes large contributions to incumbent governors who are not hostile to its interests. The company does give to individual legislators, but the number of legislators to whom it contributes is small compared to a group like the beer distributors.

The contributions made by gambling interests from 1997 to 1999 represent the most extreme example of a group pursuing a leadership-oriented, access/influence contribution strategy. Nothing big happens in the Illinois General Assembly without the active support of the legislative leaders and the governor. In addition, there is no grassroots constituency for the expansion of casino gambling. Nor is there a group of citizens that are incredibly passionate about providing tax breaks and state subsidies for horse racing. In many legislative districts, taking contributions from gambling interests would be a political liability. Yet, during the 1997-1998 election cycle, gambling interests (those in the horse racing industry, the casino industry, and those seeking casino licenses) made $1.9 million in campaign contributions. And in 1999 they gave an additional $900,000. The great majority of these contributions (more than 80 percent) went to the four legislative leaders, the incumbent, lame duck governor, a gubernatorial candidate, and the state political parties. The gambling interests wanted changes in state law, and they had the resources to make very large campaign contributions. Raising huge sums of money is a key element in the power of the legislative leaders. The details of what happened in 1999 will be examined in Chapter 5, but the strategic choice for the gambling interest as to how best to use money to gain influence in the policy process was clear: Make large contributions to leaders, and then hope for access to (and influence with) those powerful leaders.

In between the beer distributors' focus on giving to individual legislators and the gambling interests' focus on giving to the legislative leaders are groups who balance their contributions between individual members of the General Assembly and its leaders while still pursuing an access/influence-focused strategy. Among these are such corporations as Ameritech, Commonwealth Edison, and Illinois Power. No group or interest is a pure type. The beer distributors give to leaders and governors as well as individual members of the legislature. Gambling interests give to individual members in addition to legislative leaders and governors. For those in between, changes in issues, changes in leaders, or a new occupant in the Governor's Mansion may cause a shift toward giving more to members or to leaders. But, the general tendencies of all of these groups is to use money to build relationships with those in power rather than to use money to directly influence the outcome of elections.

ELECTION-ORIENTED LOBBYING STRATEGIES

A few groups try to use money to directly influence the outcome of elections. The goal is to elect candidates to office who will support the interests of the group.

But this strategy is reserved for only a few donor groups. Why? There are three primary reasons. First, the policy goals of a group may not play favorably in elections. This is certainly true of gambling, but it is also true of the CPA society. Second, the cost of trying to influence elections is extraordinary. Third, the risk of losing is a constant. If a candidate you support loses, you have nothing to show for your money except the wrath of the elected official you opposed. Of course, the upside to an election-oriented contribution strategy is that an elected official who owes his or her election to you will be very easy to lobby.

Choosing sides and coming up with enough money to make a difference in legislative or statewide elections is a daunting task. The average Senate candidate in 1998 spent $142,000 in the general election, while the average House candidate spent $92,000. There were 118 House races and 41 Senate races. Most of these races were uncontested or so obviously lopsided that the outcome was a foregone conclusion. It is only in a contested race where either major-party candidate has a reasonable chance of winning that a group can have an impact on who controls the legislature. And trying to influence every race would be impossible anyway: A group would have to raise $159,000 to give a $1,000 to a candidate in every race. While this would be useful in pursuing an access- and influence-oriented strategy, the $1,000 would not have much impact in contested races, particularly those targeted by the legislative leaders. Candidates in the 16 targeted House races in 1998 averaged $285,000 in spending, and candidates in the eight targeted Senate races averaged $360,000 in spending. So, election-oriented contributing groups choose to put many eggs into just a few baskets, opting to concentrate donation efforts on a few, key swing races and hoping that they don't back any losers.

Having chosen to use money to pursue an electoral strategy, there are still strategic choices that need to be made. Should a group focus its contributions on incumbents or challengers? Democrats or Republicans? Just legislative elections or the gubernatorial election as well? Individuals involved in legislative races, or should the group work through the legislative leaders?

The teacher unions have already been cited as groups who use money to directly influence elections as a key part of their efforts to lobby the legislative and executive branches for favorable policy decisions. Both the IEA and the IFT contribute money as well as goods and services to contested races and often provide volunteer labor to the candidates they are supporting. While both groups have similar goals and the same basic strategy for using money to gain influence, they differ in a number of ways.

The IEA stands out as one of the few major contributors to Illinois politics that does not make large contributions to the legislative leaders. It has always focused on individual members of the General Assembly and relied on their support to bring pressure to bear on the leaders. But, during the 1995-1996 and 1997-1998 election cycles, the IEA did increase its contributions to leaders of both chambers of the legislature. This is an acknowledgment of the ever-growing power of the legislative leaders over the individual members. In contrast, the IFT has always made major contributions to Democratic legislative leaders.

The IFT has been strongly partisan in its contributions, giving almost exclusively to Democrats. While the IEA gives more to Democrats than to Republicans, it is much more bipartisan than the IFT. In choosing which candidate to support, the IEA has relied on a local endorsement process that emphasizes policy agreement over party affiliation. Since the 1995-1996 legislative session, when Republicans took control of both chambers of the legislature for one term, the IFT has been more open to supporting Republican candidates. Even though the House switched back to the Democrats in 1997, the threat of being shut out of the process has not been lost on the IFT. In contrast, the IEA has always had a number of strong supporters in the House and the Senate Republican caucuses.

Another group that is election-oriented with a focus on individual members is Personal PAC, a pro-choice group. Abortion is not the kind of issue in which legislative compromise, dealmaking, or leadership pressure is likely to have an impact on what policy choices are made. The side that has a legislative majority will write the laws. The best strategy for such an issue group as this is to elect people to the legislature who support its position. Like most single-issue groups, Personal PAC is nonpartisan, supporting both pro-choice Democrats and Republicans. Also, like most single-issue groups, Personal PAC does not make contributions to the legislative leaders, who funnel contributions through their campaign funds to provide major support to candidates of their party in difficult races. Personal PAC does not want the impact of its contributions diluted or, even worse, diverted to candidates who do not support its issue. On the other hand, leaders are often reluctant to take contributions from single-issue groups for fear of having their party too closely identified with one side of a controversial issue. Pro-life and pro-choice groups are often active in legislative races in terms of volunteers and independent expenditures for fliers and mail pieces. Personal PAC is unusual for a single-issue group because it raises enough money to make significant contributions directly to candidates. But the election orientation and the single-member focus is completely consistent with its goals and circumstances. Most single-interest groups would act like Personal PAC if they had the money.

Most groups that pursue election-oriented strategies strike a balance between contributions to legislative leaders and contributions to legislators. Good examples are the Illinois Manufacturers' Association, the Illinois State AFL-CIO, the Illinois Chamber of Commerce, the Illinois State Medical Society, and the Illinois Trial Lawyers Association. All of these groups contribute to candidates in contested elections. All of them contribute to challengers as well as incumbents. All of them make large contributions to legislative leaders. All of them have a strong partisan bias. The contributions to legislative candidates made by the medical society, manufacturers' association, and state chamber overwhelmingly favor Republicans, while the contributions to legislative candidates made by the union and the trial lawyers overwhelmingly favor Democrats. The state AFL-CIO and the trial lawyers also give the vast majority of their legislative leader contributions to Democrats, while the medical society, the manufacturers, and the state chamber give the vast majority of their leadership contributions to Republicans. When a group like the Illinois State Medical Society gives money to a Democratic leader, it has nothing to do with elections. Rather, it is an acknowledgment of the power of the leaders within the process. Once the elections are over, the lobbying process begins.

Money from Individuals

Individuals contributed more than $16.6 million to legislative and statewide candidates, officeholders, and state political parties during the 1997-1998 election cycle. Nearly 26,500 individuals contributed approximately $7.8 million (47 percent) in increments of $500 or less, while 322 individuals gave $2.6 million (16 percent) in sums of $5,000 or more.

Individuals contribute to campaigns for the same reasons that groups and other entities contribute. Some want to help a friend or support a good person. Others want something specific from government, either a specific policy or program or some kind of personal gain or advantage in their relationship with government.

Analyzing the data related to individual contributions is difficult for a number of reasons. In most cases, individuals make a single contribution of $150, or $500, or $1,000 to a single candidate. As such, there are no patterns to examine. The exceptions are a small group of individuals who are regular contributors to campaigns over time and an even smaller group of very large contributors.

Prior to January 1, 1999, campaigns did not have to provide occupation or employer information for individuals who contributed. Since that date, political campaign committees are required to disclose occupation and employer information for an individual who contributes more than $500 during a six-month reporting period. Without occupation and employer information, it was impossible to make any judgments about the reasons behind a contribution. Finally, the accuracy of the reporting of contributions in Illinois often leaves a lot to be desired because there are no limits or prohibitions to worry about. Reporting a corporate contribution as coming from a corporate officer would be a serious violation of the law in a state that prohibited corporate contributions. In Illinois it only qualifies as sloppy record keeping.

Even with occupation and employer information, it is still difficult to determine the exact interest of the individual who is making a contribution. For example, James Fletcher is an attorney and a contract lobbyist. Companies, groups, and individuals hire him to represent their interests before the legislative and executive branches. He has been involved in Illinois politics for more than 30 years. He started as a legislative intern, worked on the legislative staff, and served as Governor Jim Thompson's chief of staff. He has been very active in Republican politics at the state level. During the 1997-1998 election cycle, he contributed more than $154,000 to legislative leaders, legislative candidates and officeholders, and constitutional candidates and officeholders. His law firm, Fletcher, Topal and O'Brien, gave an additional $62,000. Sorting out what portion was given to help friends, what portion was given to help the Republican Party, and what portion was given to promote the interests of his lobbying clients is an impossible task. Particularly since, in many cases, a single contribution will have the effect of advancing friendship, the Republican Party, and the interests of a client all at the same time.

Small Contributions

Candidates are not required to itemize small contributions, which are legally defined as those contributions from a single source that amount to less than $150 for a six-month reporting period. The candidates report these small contributions as a lump sum of not-itemized contributions. Therefore, it is impossible to tell where they came from. They may be contributions from individuals, from state employees, from state contractors, from individual businesses, from unions, or from associations.

For the 1997-1998 election cycle, small contributions came to more than $12 million. The most common source of these small contributions were (and are) fundraising events for which the tickets are priced at less than $150 dollars each. Many elected officials hold fundraising events in their districts on a regular basis. The amount of not-itemized contributions reported by incumbent state legislators for a six-month period range from zero to more than $63,000. The amount of not-itemized contributions reported by the governor and other statewide officials can exceed half a million dollars for a six-month period. Governor Jim Edgar announced in fall 1997 that he would not run for re-election. He still raised more than $409,000 in not-itemized contributions in 1997.

It is often assumed that a large percentage of the not-itemized contributions reported by statewide officials, particularly the governor and the secretary of state, represent contributions from state employees who have purchased tickets to fundraising events. Before taking office, Governor-elect George Ryan announced that he was no longer accepting contributions from executive branch employees as of January 1, 1999. A comparison of the not-itemized contributions he raised during the nonelection year of 1997, when Ryan was secretary of state and still accepting contributions from executive branch employees, with what he reported for the nonelection year of 1999, when he no longer took contributions from those employees, is very suggestive. For the two reporting periods in calendar year 1997, then-Secretary of State George Ryan reported $626,509 in not-itemized contributions. For the two reporting periods in calendar year 1999, with the ban on contributions for state employees in effect, Governor Ryan reported a total of $2,085 in not-itemized contributions. In 1999, Secretary of State Jesse White raised more than $148,000 in not-itemized contributions. The huge decline in not-itemized contributions to Governor Ryan and the continued large amount raised by Secretary of State White, who still accepted contributions from executive branch employees, strongly suggests that contributions from state employees have been and continue to be a major source of not-itemized contributions for statewide officials.

Money from Political Sources

Illinois does not limit the size of contributions to the political committees of candidates, officeholders, or political parties at either the local or state level. Nor is there a limit on how much money can be transferred from one political committee to another. As a result, more than one out of every five dollars contributed to legislative and statewide candidates and elected officials in Illinois in the 1997-1998 election cycle came from other candidates or elected officials. In targeted, heavily competitive legislative races, the figure is more than six out of every ten dollars. Money from political sources plays a critical role in the election process, and the financial clout of the legislative leaders in elections in Illinois is well-documented. Both of these relationships will be examined in detail in Chapters 4 and 5.

While Illinois politicians are a very resourceful and creative group of individuals, they have not yet figured out how to print their own money. All of the money that flows through the Illinois political system starts out as private money. Some individual, corporation, union, group, or association starts the process by writing a check or providing goods and services to a political committee. That money becomes political money when it is transferred to the political committee of another candidate or elected official.

While political money is recycled private money, treating it as a separate part of the total amount of money flowing through the political system is not engaging in double counting. Consider the following example. In the 1997-1998 election cycle, Michael Madigan, the speaker of the House, raised more than $4 million. The public employees' union (AFSCME) contributed $181,000, the hotel and restaurant employees' union (TIP) contributed $162,000, and the Illinois Hospital and HealthSystems Association (IHHA) contributed $102,000. The total for the three groups came to $445,000. In the 1998 general election period, political committees controlled by Speaker Madigan contributed slightly more than $400,000 to the campaign of Greg Backes, who lost his race for the House seat in the 107th District in southeastern Illinois. From an accounting standpoint, the total amount of money that came into the political system is $445,000, not $845,000. However, from the practical perspective of the participants, two relationships have been created, and $845,000 has changed hands. One relationship is between the interest groups and Speaker Madigan. The other is a $400,000 relationship between the speaker and a legislative candidate. The legislative candidate sees only leader money, not recycled union and hospital association money. Now let's say that candidate Backes had won that House seat. With $400,000 in backing from the speaker, one wonders how free Backes would have felt to vote against the speaker's wishes on any hotly contested legislative issue to come before the House.

Sources of Political Money

The political money that flows into the political committees of legislative leaders, legislators and legislative candidates, and statewide constitutional officeholders and candidates for statewide office comes from all levels of the Illinois political system. There is township and ward party money, county party money, legislative chamber committee money, and state party money. Money comes from township and ward committeemen; from mayors, aldermen, and county board members; from legislators and legislative leaders; and from constitutional officers. In some cases, there is money from national party organizations. In all, a total of $21.2 million was transferred from one political committee to another during the 1997-1998 election cycle. That represented almost 20 percent of the total money in the political system. That portion was consistent with the pattern for the rest of the 1990s.

By far, the largest amount of political money comes from the legislative leaders and legislative chamber committees and is transferred to legislative candidates running in races that have been targeted by the leaders. In the 1998 general election period, legislative leaders transferred almost $10 million to targeted legislative races.

Incumbent legislators provided an additional $660,000 to candidates in targeted races, while county parties were a distant third with $58,000 in transfers.

Part of the pool of money from which legislative leaders made transfers to candidates in targeted legislative races came from other political sources. The legislative leaders themselves received $729,000 from incumbent legislators during the 1997-1998 election cycle. They also received over $300,000 from constitutional officers and $225,000 from national party organizations.

In turn, constitutional officer candidates also received political money. More than $1 million from the two state political parties and $960,000 from incumbent legislators was transferred to candidates for governor and other constitutional offices. An additional $780,000 from local and county party organizations and $190,000 from national party organizations was transferred to candidates for statewide office.

The Motivations for Contributing Political Money

The primary reason for raising money through one political committee and transferring it to another political committee is straightforward and obvious: power. The legislative leaders and incumbent legislators from the two party caucuses in the Senate want to win a majority of the seats in the Senate. The same is true of the legislative leaders and incumbent legislators from the two party caucuses in the House. Governors want their party to have control of the legislature and to have influence over members of the legislature. Democratic Party officials at the local, county, and state level want to elect Democrats at all levels, and their Republican counterparts want to elect Republicans.

There are certainly differences in how people want that power to be used once the election is over. For some, the ultimate goals may be policy and programs. Democratic control of the legislature or the governor's office means one set of policies and programs. Republican control would mean another. For others, the goal of winning is to get access to jobs, contracts, and personal gain. And for others, getting and exercising power is a goal in and of itself. Whatever the goal, winning elections is a means to an end or is an end itself.

In addition to winning for partisan reasons, individual incumbent legislators may be motivated by friendship to make contributions to other legislators. A good example would be legislators' attending each other's golf outing fundraisers during the summer.

Personal ambition may motivate others to raise and transfer money to other politicians. A legislator who anticipates an opening in the leadership of his or her caucus may raise money and transfer it to other legislators in order to build goodwill or to demonstrate fundraising ability and leadership skills. The hope is that these gestures to other legislators can be translated into support when a new leader is being chosen. The same would be true for a legislator who is thinking about running for statewide office or a constitutional officer planning to run for governor.

Contribution Strategies for Political Money

Transferring money or goods and services to a candidate from another political committee raises two strategic considerations. First, who will control the spending, the giver or the one receiving the transfer? Second, what will be the public and media reaction if the transfer becomes public knowledge?

When a state representative buys a $250 ticket to a state senator's golf outing, there is no concern on the part of the state representative as to how that money will be used. Similarly, if a state senator gives a $5,000 contribution to a colleague facing a more difficult re-election campaign than usual, there would be no expectation that the giver would be consulted as to how the money is to be spent. However, if a legislative leader is going to invest $200,000 to $500,000 in support of a candidate for the legislature, it is unlikely that a check will arrive from Springfield along with just a note wishing the candidate good luck.

The 1990s pattern in targeted legislative races is for the legislative leaders to run the campaigns. Rather than transfer cash, the typical approach is for the leader to use a party committee, usually a legislative chamber committee, to pay for campaign staff, polling, mailing, and electronic media. These are all reported by the candidate as in-kind contributions, but control over how the campaign is run rests with the candidate's legislative leader. The involvement of governors and other constitutional officers in targeted legislative races has generally been one of simply transferring money or putting together a media endorsement and paying to have it shown. Occasionally, a constitutional officer will work a legislative campaign more directly by providing staff or services, but statewide officials leave the overall control with the legislative candidate or, in the case of a targeted race, with the candidate's legislative leader.

In statewide campaigns, there can be large transfers from legislative and party committees to campaigns. Legislative and party committees may also provide goods and services such as polling, direct mail, and media. In all cases, the control of the spending and the day-to-day operation of the campaigns for statewide offices have remained with the candidates.

If the Republican candidate in a targeted legislative race gets 65 percent of his funding from the Republican leader and the Democratic candidate gets 70 percent of her funding from the legislative leader, the candidates are not likely to start a debate about who is more obligated to his or her leader or who is more reliant on money from outside the district. Still, the question of appearances has led, over time, to some variations in the mechanics of how transfers are made to candidates in targeted legislative races. Control of those campaigns, however, has remained in the hands of the leaders.

Leaders have two large sources of political money at their disposal. First, they have their own campaign fund. Since leaders are in safe districts, they often don't need lots of money to win re-election. So, they can transfer their campaign money into the kitties of those candidates who need more. Second, three of the four leaders also have control of a legislative chamber committee fund. For example, House Minority Leader Lee Daniels has total authority over the House Republican Campaign Committee. (The exception among the leaders is House Speaker Michael Madigan. After a dispute with the United States Postal Service, the House Democrats closed their chamber committee in early 1997.)

General election transfers from a legislative leader to a targeted race will be made primarily from a party committee such as a legislative chamber committee. The situation is different in contested legislative primaries. At least lip service is paid to the idea that these are local decisions in which the party committees at the legislative level are neutral. When a legislative leader is supporting a candidate in a contested primary for a legislative seat, the support will be paid out of the leader's political committee rather than out of a legislative chamber committee.

Since Speaker of the House Michael Madigan became state Democratic Party chairman in 1998, there has been a shift in how transfers are made for Democratic candidates in targeted legislative races. In the 1998 general election, money was transferred from the political funds of the two Democratic legislative leaders and the Senate Democratic chamber committee to the state Democratic Party. The state Democratic Party then transferred money and paid for goods and services for the Democratic candidates in the targeted races.

In the 1998 campaign for governor, Democrat Glenn Poshard imposed a limit on contributions from individuals and did not accept contributions from political action committees. This ban did not apply to contributions from political committees. Incumbent Democratic House members contributed almost $375,000 to Poshard's campaign. Incumbent Democratic Senate members gave an additional $92,000. The state Democratic Party contributed $843,000 to Poshard's campaign, while county and local political parties contributed another $350,000. Poshard also received $67,000 from the two Democratic legislative leaders. In contrast, the Republican candidate, George Ryan, received $92,000 from incumbent House members and $51,000 from incumbent Senate members. He received $61,000 from the two Republican legislative leaders. While he received less than $2,000 from the state Republican Party, Ryan received $175,000 from the Republican National Committee. Though both candidates benefited from the lack of restrictions on transfers from one political committee to another, the Democratic Party used legislative political committees and the state party committee to get resources to Poshard, while not technically violating the limits that Poshard chose to impose on his own campaign.

Money Is Money — And Money Counts

In Illinois politics, money is money. Distinctions that complicate the campaign finance debate at the federal level — hard vs. soft money, independent vs. coordinated expenditures — do not apply. Once money comes into the Illinois system from a private source as a specific contribution to a specific candidate, it loses that identity. Once money is transferred from one political committee to another, it changes identity again. There is unlimited freedom to take money and redirect it or recycle it. As we'll see in the following chapters, the possibilities for creativity and mischief are endless.

So Many Dollars, So Few Races

Money and Elections in Illinois

The recipe for elephant stew begins with these instructions:
"First, take one elephant."

Faced with the task of making elephant stew, most of us would have no idea where to get an elephant. Of course, even having an elephant would not guarantee that we could cook up a batch, but it's certain that a luncheon of elephant stew requires at least one pachyderm. Winning a competitive election in Illinois is like making elephant stew, except that the key ingredient is money. Finding the money to run for office is difficult, particularly for the novice. And having money won't guarantee victory, but you can't win without it.

In general, it takes money — a lot of money — to win and hold public office in Illinois. In 1998, George Ryan spent $9.8 million[1] in the general election to win the governor's race. The losing candidate, Glenn Poshard, spent $3.6 million. Figure 4.1 tells the story of costs associated with running for a General Assembly seat. A candidate for a seat in the Illinois House in 1998 spent an average of $92,000. On average, a candidate for the Senate spent $142,000. The most spent by a House candidate was $468,000, while the most spent by a Senate candidate was $778,000. Combined spending in one Senate race exceeded $1.3 million. The winning candidate in one Supreme Court district spent more than $500,000 in the 2000 primary, while one losing candidate spent more than $1.5 million, and another spent more than $1 million. In another Supreme Court district, the winning candidate spent more than $1 million, as did the candidate who finished fourth.

If you are a candidate who is not independently wealthy and you don't have a lot of rich friends, then your only option is to become friends with individuals, groups, or entities that have money. One of

---

[1]All dollar figures, unless otherwise noted, were generated from an Illinois campaign finance database created by the author. Support for the database was provided by The Joyce Foundation and the Institute for Public Affairs at the University of Illinois at Springfield. The database contains receipt and expenditure records beginning with January 1, 1993, and is updated every six months. As of August 2000, the database contained more than 400,000 records from more than 600 candidates for legislative and statewide offices.

FIGURE 4.1

Running for the General Assembly

HOUSE RACES

GENERAL ELECTION	1994	1996	1998
Average spending by a candidate	$70,000	$87,000	$92,000
Most spent by a candidate	$393,000	$485,000	$468,000
Least spent by a winning candidate	$12,000	$5,000	$12,000
Cost of the ten most expensive races	$5.38 million	$7.19 million	$7.06 million
Races with combined spending $700,000	1	7	6
# of incumbents seeking election	105 of 118	108 of 118	103 of 118
# of incumbents elected	91	101	102
Incumbent election rate	87%	94%	99%

UNITS IN $1 THOUSAND

Average spent by candidate in targeted race

Average spent by winners in nontargeted race

Average spent by losers in nontargeted race

SENATE RACES

GENERAL ELECTION	1994	1996	1998
Average spending by a candidate	$101,000	$134,000	$142,000
Most spent by a candidate	$789,000	$758,000	$778,000
Least spent by a winning candidate	$16,000	$22,000	$16,000
Cost of the five most expensive races	$3.16 million	$5.29 million	$4.52 million
Races with combined spending $1 million	1	4	2
# of incumbents seeking election	19 of 21	37 of 40	39 of 41
# of incumbents elected	18	35	37
Incumbent election rate	95%	95%	95%

UNITS IN $1 THOUSAND

Average spent by candidate in targeted race

Average spent by winners in nontargeted race

Average spent by losers in nontargeted race

the reasons incumbents are so difficult to beat is that they make these kinds of friends a lot more easily than challengers do.

Chapter 3 dealt with who these potential friends are and why they want to be friends with candidates for public office and elected officials. This chapter deals with the impact of money on elections. We will look specifically at the impact of money on elections for the legislature, the governor's office and the other constitutional officers, and judges at the appellate and Supreme Court levels. The next chapter will deal with the impact of money on making public policy.

Can Money Buy Happiness?

Any time a candidate for political office spends what appears to be a lot of money, concerns will be voiced, in campaign rhetoric or editorial opinion, that so-and-so is trying to "buy" the election. Can you buy an election? Just what does money do and not do for a candidate?

In general, voters refuse to cast ballots for people they don't know. The exception is the partisan voter who votes for every candidate on the basis of his or her party label. For the rest of the electorate, in order to win a vote, a candidate must first be perceived. He or she has to be on the radar screen. Elections between the well-known incumbent Smith and the unknown challenger Jones are almost never contests.

Some voters cast votes on the basis of a single issue. They want to identify and vote for the anti-abortion candidate, the green candidate, the no-tax candidate, or no-nuke candidate. But for most voters, the choice is both more complex and less focused. Their general impression of the candidates in a race comes from a mixture of substance and style, with some level of party preference thrown in as historical context. So, candidates need to enter the voters' consciousness not only by being perceived, but by being perceived positively. The positive attribution can stand alone, as in: "Smith is a good person." Or it can be comparative, as in: "Smith would not be nearly as bad as Jones." A contest between the well-known *and* "beloved, hard-working, right-thinking" incumbent Smith and the unknown challenger Jones is absolutely no contest.

Elected public officials have the opportunity to become well-known and to do positive things for their constituents by virtue of holding office and performing their official duties. They can make public appearances, handle constituents' problems, and take credit for concrete goods and services provided by government, such as roads and bridges, flood relief, and economic development grants. They can take public positions in favor of "good" things: better schools, less crime, cleaner air, etc. If incumbents work at being visible and doing positive things, they can be known — and positively perceived — in ways that have nothing to do with being Democrats or Republicans, or with voting for or against a particular piece of legislation, or with how much money they raise.

The candidate with high name recognition and a strong public identity (e.g., former Vice President Dan Quayle) does not need to spend money becoming more well-known. And, in the case of Quayle, it is questionable whether or not spending a lot of money to change his public perception ever would be successful. Beyond a certain point, every extra dollar spent by the well-known incumbent produces ever-diminishing returns.

For the unknown candidate, becoming known and establishing an identity is both an opportunity and a challenge. The candidate has the opportunity to define herself to the voters. The challenge is to find the right message and methods of communication and then sufficient resources to communicate that identity to those voters. It takes a certain level of resources to be visible as a candidate, to be on the radar screen for regular, attentive voters and the news media. Most challengers who face incumbent Illinois legislators in politically safe districts are invisible. It seems only their immediate families are aware they are running. Given the power of incumbency, becoming visible in most legislative races means that the candidate loses with 30 percent of the vote instead of 10 percent of the vote. (The candidate still loses, but the visibility may help him for another race.) The first challenge for any legislative candidate is to become visible.

The nonincumbent, particularly the challenger to an incumbent, typically lacks every resource the incumbent has: name recognition, opportunities to provide service to constituents, identification with government programs and services, a seasoned campaign organization with plenty of human resources, and a big campaign war chest. It takes money to become known enough for a candidate's image and message to reach a critical mass. It takes even more resources to become viable, that is, to be seen as having a chance by regular voters and the news media and to be on the radar screen of people who vote only occasionally.

Money is a means to an end. Money can be the great equalizer. The development of modern campaign technology allows a candidate to substitute capital for labor or to substitute capital for political experience and name recognition. It can buy direct mail pieces, media ads, telephone calls, polls, and campaign staff. And these resources, with the right candidate and the right message, can provide the name recognition and the public identity a candidate needs to become visible, then viable, and even, maybe, victorious.

Visibility is the first challenge for most candidates for statewide office running in their party primaries. The next challenge — viability — requires both substance and the resources to get the candidate and the message before the voters. The primary winners for governor and secretary of state will receive enough media attention to maintain visibility without a huge amount of additional resources. Candidates for state treasurer or comptroller don't get as much free, visibility-building media coverage. They will have a difficult time maintaining visibility unless they have the money or the name recognition to present a strong, statewide campaign. The natural visibility factor for candidates for the state attorney general's race is somewhere between the governor's race and the comptroller's.

However, some campaigns are not winnable — and some candidates are not electable — no matter how much money the loser spends. A well-funded candidate with a good message and a strategically sound campaign is unlikely to defeat an incumbent in a district where the challenger's political party is outnumbered three to one. And no amount of money will overcome a bad candidate, a bad message, or a bad campaign, particularly if the candidate is challenging an incumbent. If an incumbent is in real political trouble, either from bad votes or bad behavior, then even the incumbent's advantage of being able to raise big money may not be enough to compensate. Every election cycle, some of the highest spending losing candidates are unsuccessful incumbents. They can raise money, but money cannot make them more well-known, and money cannot deliver a message to voters who have stopped listening. Illinois Democratic Congressman Dan Rostenkowski's 1994 loss in a very Democratic district to unknown Republican challenger Michael Patrick Flanagan is a case in point. The voters' reaction to Rostenkowski's ethical problems was to "throw the rascal out."

How much money a candidate needs is really a threshold question because money is one of a number of resources (including incumbency, party organization, celebrity status, personal characteristics, experience, charisma, and powerful symbolic issues) that a candidate can draw upon to run for office. The candidate with incumbency, a strong party organization, a favorable election district, a positive public identity, and a voting record that is responsive to local concerns does not need a lot of money to win re-election. These candidates are more than viable without spending a dime to get re-elected, and a minimal effort will make them invincible. Typically, though, safe incumbents will raise much more than they need to win. They do this, in part, because a big campaign war chest can discourage opponents from even running, and the best opponent is no opponent. Safe incumbents also will raise a lot of money with very little effort because groups that want access to power will contribute to them regardless of how easily they will be able to win re-election.

For the challenger facing an incumbent, or a candidate making a run for an open seat, getting outspent two to one is not necessarily fatal, if that "one" is big enough. Candidates need enough resources to get noticed so they can get the substance of their campaigns out to the public. (As we've seen, that's how unknowns become viable.) The problem is that the cost of being viable in Illinois keeps going up. Running a credible campaign against an incumbent takes at least $150,000 for a seat in the Illinois House of Representatives. In 1998, eight challengers in House races spent more than $300,000 each and still lost to incumbent members.

Yet, how much a candidate spends in total and who spends the most is a rough predictor of election success. Candidates who spend a lot and spend more than their opponents are more likely to win. And how strong a candidate runs in an election can be a function of how much money she spends. Money is that important. A good candidate with a good message and good strategy still needs money to win. It may not be sufficient, but it is necessary. And the absence of money? That is usually fatal, particularly for the challenger or the newcomer struggling to get over the visibility threshold.

Party-Centered Campaigns and Candidate-Centered Campaigns

Historically, political parties were at the center of the American electoral process. They recruited the candidates. They raised the money. They ran the campaigns. They got out the vote. The model of a party-centered electoral process in Illinois has always been Cook County elections as orchestrated by the political machine of the late Chicago Mayor Richard J. Daley. Those days are gone. Most observers of Illinois politics acknowledge the decline of the power of state and local political parties over the past three decades.

Politics, like nature, abhors a vacuum. Candidate-centered electoral processes have been both the beneficiary and partial cause of the declining role of parties in elections. Open primaries; modern, media-oriented campaigns; computer-based campaign technology, including polling, targeting, and direct mail; and political action committees have all contributed to a shift away from parties and toward candidates as the focus of elections. The shift away from party-centered campaigns at the state level in Illinois is symbolized by Dan Walker's 1972 Democratic gubernatorial primary victory over Paul Simon, the candidate of Chicago Mayor Richard J. Daley and the state Democratic Party, as well as by Walker's subsequent victory in the general election. Walker recruited himself. He raised his own money, formed his own campaign organization, and made himself the focus of a modern, media-oriented campaign.

The power of a party-centered campaign can be seen in the 1976 Democratic gubernatorial primary in which Mayor Daley used the Cook County Democratic Machine to turn out enough votes to deny Governor Walker the renomination. Michael Howlett, the popular secretary of state, was nominated in his place. But, the triumph was short-lived. Turning Howlett's long career in politics and his ties to the Cook County Democratic Party against him, the Republican candidate, James R. Thompson, ran as a crusading former federal prosecutor ready to sweep out the old politics of Illinois' past. Howlett suffered a humiliating defeat, illustrating the limitations of a party-centered statewide campaign in the era of candidate-centered politics.

Candidate-centered processes — self-recruitment, building a personal campaign organization, using computerized campaign technology, sending personally produced direct mail pieces, running a media-oriented campaign focusing on the candidate, and grabbing interest-group campaign contributions — have become the staple of statewide elections in Illinois. But the picture for legislative elections is more complex. While candidate-centered campaigns are the norm in safe districts, the role of the legislative leaders in competitive districts produces elections that are strongly in the party-centered campaign model. In either case, a candidate with money can buy what political parties cannot or will not provide. In the absence of a strong party organization, the candidate without money is at a serious disadvantage.

The Different Worlds of Legislative Elections

We know a good deal about the role of money in legislative elections in Illinois. There are a lot of legislative elections. They take place frequently. All 118 House members run every two years. Depending on the election, either one-third or two-thirds of the 59 Senate seats will be up. In the election after the redistricting that occurs every decade, every House and Senate seat is up for election. Statewide private sector interests, statewide political forces, and the news media consider legislative elections important.

The story of the financing of legislative elections in Illinois is really the story of the two very different worlds in which those elections take place. The largest world of Illinois legislative elections is one where the well-financed, winning candidates — often incumbents — run unopposed or run against weak opponents who spend little or no money. In the 1994, 1996, and 1998 elections, more than 74 percent of the winning candidates in House races, on average, had no opponent or an opponent who spent less than $50,000 or who received less than 40 percent of the vote. In Senate races during those same three elections, the winners had no opponent or a weak opponent more than 71 percent of the time (see Table 4.1).

TABLE 4.1

Competitiveness for Seats
in the Illinois General Assembly

	HOUSE			SENATE		
	1994	1996	1998	1994	1996	1998
Number of seats up	118	118	118	21	40	41
Number unopposed	35	31	58	7	16	21
Number with weak opponents	52	56	31	9	13	7
Number that were competitive	7	11	13	0	4	5
Number targeted by leaders	24	20	16	5	7	8

In most of the districts where the winner has little or no opposition, one political party dominates. How much money a challenger from the minority party raises in these districts is almost irrelevant. In some districts there appears to be a more partisan balance, yet the winning candidate faces little or no competition election after election. These districts are usually represented by a longtime incumbent with a huge campaign war chest, making it very difficult for a challenger to raise money and even more difficult for that challenger to win. In the Illinois world of longtime incumbents and safe districts, incumbents never lose and open seats held by one party never change hands.

The second, smaller, world of legislative elections is one of contested elections. In general, these are elections in which the losing candidate will spend more than $50,000 or receive at least 40 percent of the vote. The highest profile contested races are those elections targeted by the legislative leaders. These contests are dominated by support from the legislative leaders and a few powerful interest groups with large amounts of resources to put into political campaigns. By definition, these are races in which one or both of the legislative leaders has made a strong financial commitment ($100,000 or more) to a candidate. The number of targeted legislative races in any election is very small. In 1994, 1996, and 1998, an average of only 17 percent of House races and 20 percent of Senate races fell into the targeted category. When incumbent legislators lose or open seats shift from one party to the other, it is almost always in this type of election.

Between uncontested elections and targeted races is a gray area of contested, competitive elections in which neither candidate receives any significant assistance from a legislative leader. In 1994, 1996, and 1998, only about nine percent of either House or Senate races fell into this category. Races in this category may be competitive in terms of the amount of money raised by one or both candidates or in terms of the vote, with the loser gaining more than 40 percent of the vote. While incumbent legislators do not lose in this type of race, open seats occasionally can produce changes in political party control of the district.

So, a race for a seat in the General Assembly from Chicago may be a completely different animal than a race for a seat in the General Assembly from Cairo. At issue is competitiveness, and competitiveness is a factor of political geography, incumbency of candidates, ability to generate financial support, and party leaders' decision to target the race.

How a Legislative Race Becomes a Contest

Why do Illinois legislative elections — and the spending on those elections — tend to split along two lines, the contested versus the uncontested? The answer begins with the way that the legislative district maps are drawn. Every 10 years, it is the legislature's responsibility to create a new set of legislative districts that take into account population changes in the state over the past decade. Legislative districts must be equal in population. They also must be compact and contiguous, and they cannot be designed for the purpose of diluting the voting strength of minority populations. The General Assembly has until June 30 of the year following each federal census to pass a new legislative map that the governor will sign. If the process fails in that time frame, then the responsibility for drawing a new map shifts to a commission of eight members, two appointed by the each of the four legislative leaders. This results in a commission with four members from each political party. If no compromise is reached, control of that committee ultimately is established by choosing a ninth member by lot who is either a Democrat or a Republican. This lottery process occurred in 1981, when the Democrats won control of the commission, and again in 1991, when the Republicans won control.

Faced with the broad options of drawing as many competitive districts as possible or as many safe districts as possible, the general strategy in 1981 and 1991 was for the legislative leaders of the party in control to draw as many safe districts as possible for both parties, while structuring the districts that were competitive to favor the party that controlled the process. Given the political geography of the state, this strategy makes sense. It is unlikely that Republican candidates will win, or even run, in overwhelmingly Democratic districts in the heart of Chicago. The same is true for Democratic candidates in heavily Republican districts in DuPage County. It is even more unlikely that legislative leaders or interest groups will contribute or spend money in support of any quixotic candidate in those areas.

Illinois has single-member Senate districts that cover the same territory as two single-member House districts. This creates a conflict during redistricting even among the party that controls the process because those representing the Senate side want to create a set of 59 Senate districts that are most favorable to their interests and then divide each of those 59 Senate districts into two House districts. Those representing the House side want to create a set of 118 House districts that give them the most electoral advantage and then combine them into 59 Senate districts. This focus on the prospects of each party group in each chamber carries over into elections. Each of the four legislative leaders and chamber groups is primarily concerned with partisan control of its chamber.

In geographic areas where the partisan division among voters is more even, who controls the mapmaking process can be the major factor in determining which party is successful in winning the subsequent elections. For instance, in 1981 the Democrats drew largely urban districts around Springfield, Decatur, and Champaign-Urbana. These districts elected Democrats throughout the ten-year existence of that legislative map. In 1991, the Republicans eliminated these downstate urban districts, splitting the territory in the cities and adding rural areas that were expected to favor Republican candidates. The result has been mixed, but the net result after the 1998 election was a gain of two Republican seats within the same geographic area covered by the 1981 map.

Under both the 1981 and 1991 maps, there were large portions of the state made up of safe districts for one or the other of the two political parties. Under both maps, there were (and are) natural battleground areas where candidates from either party might win. The essence of good mapmaking, from a partisan standpoint, is to draw districts in those competitive areas that give your party an advantage in terms of the partisan makeup of the districts. All of this results in a large number of safe districts with relatively inexpensive elections and a small number of competitive districts that usually have very expensive elections. The new legislative map drawn in 2001 for the 2002 elections will have the same basic character, regardless of who controls the process.

The second reason legislative elections tend to divide into a large group of uncontested elections and a smaller group of contested elections is the power of legislative leaders to target specific contests. As noted in Chapters 2 and 3, the campaign finance law in Illinois allows any political committee to raise unlimited funds and then transfer them to another campaign. The legislative leaders use their positions to raise huge sums of money that they then redirect to legislative races. Leaders and access-oriented contributors usually will view a district dominated by the opposite party as a bad risk for gaining a seat, even when there is no incumbent running for re-election. The legislative leaders will view most challengers to incumbents as bad risks, even if they are in potentially competitive districts. This leaves a very few districts where the partisan balance and the relative strength of the incumbent (or the absence of an incumbent) combine to create an opportunity to take a seat from the other party and to shift the balance of power in the legislative chamber. These contests, then, become the focus of political leaders. Money from interest groups with a partisan slant will follow leadership money into these targeted district races.

The third reason legislative elections tend to divide into a large group of uncontested elections and a smaller group of contested elections already has been alluded to: the power of incumbency. Interest groups seeking access to power, particularly interests who are status quo-oriented, give money to those already in power. These groups have no reason to give money to a challenger trying to beat an incumbent or to a non-incumbent trying to win an open seat. Giving money to incumbents who are sure winners in no-contest elections or to incumbents who are likely to win in moderately contested elections is an effective strategy for these groups. In this atmosphere, incumbents know that they almost always can raise a substantial amount of money from interests seeking access. Incumbents also have past experience at winning public office. Both of these factors usually make giving to incumbents a good strategic choice for private interests who want to gain or maintain access to whomever is in power.

Another advantage of incumbency is that it depresses opposition, even in potentially competitive districts. A good example is the 100th Illinois House District, which covers a large portion of Springfield. It leans Republican, but not overwhelmingly so. In 1992 and 1994, it hosted key targeted races, with the Democratic and Republican legislative leaders and key interest groups spending heavily on both sides. The Republican candidate, Gwenn Klingler, won narrowly in 1994 in a race with combined spending of $540,000. In 1996, she won comfortably in a race with combined spending of more than $777,000. In 1998, the Democrats fielded only a token candidate who received no support from the Democratic legislative leader. And no Democrat even bothered to run in the 2000 primary. The basic political demographics of the district have not changed, but with a three-term incumbent it is no longer a good strategic opportunity for the Democrats. This pattern has been repeated over the past decade for both Democratic and Republican legislators in a number of House and Senate districts.

Targeted Legislative Races:
Leaders Rush in and So Does the Money

In every election cycle there are a few hyperexpensive, hotly contested legislative races. These are the targeted races. They stand in stark contrast to the large majority of legislative races, which are uncontested or undercontested. Targeted races are, as the term suggests, those races that have been targeted by either or both of the chamber leaders of the legislative parties of the candidates. In these races, the leaders coordinate the traditional roles played by political parties. Where there is no incumbent, they recruit the candidate. They raise the majority of the money for the candidate they are supporting. Either directly or indirectly, they organize and run the campaign for the candidate they support.

In each election, there are generally five to 12 Senate races and 16 to 24 House races that are seriously contested by one or both of the legislative leaders (see Table 4.2). Which seats are targeted rests on two factors that have already been discussed: political geography and incumbency. For a leader to commit $300,000 to $400,000 or more to a race, the district has to have some degree of partisan balance. The best candidate and all the money in the world will not make much of a dent in a district with a 70-30 party split. If a popular incumbent represents that district, the chances of a successful challenge are absolute zero. However, a 55-45 district with no incumbent or with an incumbent in trouble at least will catch the attention of the legislative leader of the district's minority party. This, the leader will think, is an opportunity to pick up a seat. On the other hand, such a district will be a serious concern for the legislative leader of the district's majority party, who will be worried about losing a district the party already holds. Those few districts with even party splits and a history of successful challenges will remain targets election after election.

As shown in Table 4.2, the overall trend for the decade has been dramatic. The amount spent by both candidates in a targeted House race doubled between 1992 and 1996, while the amount spent by

TABLE 4.2

Targeted Races:
General Election Spending by Both Candidates

	HOUSE		SENATE	
	AVERAGE SPENT	NUMBER OF RACES	AVERAGE SPENT	NUMBER OF RACES
1992	$251,000	23 of 118	$454,000	12 of 59
1994	$401,000	24 of 118	$594,000	5 of 21
1996	$582,000	20 of 118	$835,000	7 of 40
1998	$572,000	16 of 118	$728,000	8 of 41

both candidates in a targeted Senate race increased 84 percent. The average amount of spending in targeted races leveled off in 1998, due to a decrease in the quantity and quality of the opportunities for picking up or losing seats. After three elections under the same legislative map, fewer districts were in play and not all of them received an all-out effort from the leader to support a challenger. But, records for spending were still set in the House in 1998 with two races approaching $850,000 each.

The amount of support provided by the legislative leaders to their candidates in targeted districts is staggering. Collectively the four legislative leaders raised $18.5 million in the 1997-1998 election cycle, down slightly from the previous cycle. They transferred a good chunk of that money to candidates running in targeted districts. As Table 4.3 shows, the $215,000 average of cash and services from House Republican leader Lee Daniels accounted for 67 percent of the spending by House Republican candidates in 16 targeted races in 1998. House Speaker Michael Madigan provided, on average, $171,000, or 68 percent, of the amount spent by Democratic candidates running in those same districts. Senate President James "Pate" Philip came up with an average $295,000 in cash and services for Republican candidates in eight targeted Senate races in 1998. That's equal to 68 percent of the amount those candidates spent. Senate Democratic leader Emil Jones put an average of $158,000 into the campaign funds of each of the Democratic candidates in those same districts, which accounted for 54 percent of the money they spent.

TABLE 4.3

Average Leadership Contribution
to Candidates in Targeted Races

1998 GENERAL ELECTION

	AVERAGE TOTAL EXPENDITURES	AVERAGE LEADERSHIP CONTRIBUTION	LEADERSHIP CONTRIBUTION AS A PERCENTAGE OF TOTAL EXPENDITURES
House (16 races)			
Republican	$319,000	$215,000	67%
Democrat	$253,000	$171,000	68%
TOTAL	$572,000	$386,000	67%
Senate (8 races)			
Republican	$435,000	$295,000	68%
Democrat	$293,000	$158,000	54%
TOTAL	$728,000	$453,000	62%

The most expensive targeted legislative races in 1998 (see Table 4.4) illustrate the dominance of the legislative leaders in financing targeted races. The 58th Senate District is in deep southern Illinois. In terms of per capita income, it ranks in the bottom third of Senate districts. The two candidates for the 58th Senate seat spent a total of $1,337,000 in the general election. That is just $4,000 short of the record set by the same two candidates two years earlier. The incumbent, Republican Senator David Luechtefeld, spent $778,000, of which $581,000 (75 percent) came from political committees controlled by the Senate president. He won with 55 percent of the vote. The Democratic challenger, Barb Brown, spent $559,000 and got 45 percent of the vote. The Senate minority leader provided $382,000 (68 percent of her support).

The 106th House District is in far east central Illinois along the Indiana border. In terms of per capita income, it ranks in the bottom third of House districts. In the 106th District, the two candidates spent $850,000 in the general election, a new record. Dale Righter, the incumbent Republican representative who had been appointed to the seat a year earlier, spent $440,000, of which $315,000 (72 percent) came from the House minority leader. He got 57 percent of the vote. The losing Democratic candidate, Carolyn Brown Hodge, spent $410,000, of which $340,000 (83 percent) came from the speaker of the House.

TABLE 4.4

Most Expensive Legislative Races

1998 GENERAL ELECTION

	TOTAL EXPENDITURES		LEADER CONTRIBUTION
19TH SENATE DISTRICT			
William Mahar (R)(I)	$612,000	(W)	$424,000
Pam Woodward (D)	$391,000		$255,000
TOTAL	$1,003,000		$679,000
58TH SENATE DISTRICT			
David Luechtefeld (R)(I)	$778,000	(W)	$581,000
Barb Brown (D)	$559,000		$382,000
TOTAL	$1,337,000		$963,000
106TH HOUSE DISTRICT *NEW HOUSE RECORD!*			
Dale Righter (R)(I)	$440,000	(W)	$315,000
Carolyn Brown Hodge (D)	$410,000		$340,000
TOTAL	$850,000		$655,000
107TH HOUSE DISTRICT			
John Jones (R)(I)	$381,000	(W)	$261,000
Greg Backes (D)	$468,000		$401,000
TOTAL	$849,000		$662,000

W=Won
I=Incumbent

But the leaders do much more than write checks to candidates. The leaders all maintain staffs in Springfield that go off the state payroll every election year to become the core of large campaign organizations. These organizations coordinate each party caucus's election effort. In most cases, leadership staff members actually run the day-to-day operations of the campaigns for candidates in targeted races, particularly for non-incumbents. The leadership staffs will do polling, generate voter lists, and organize other general support activities for their candidates. They also will develop and produce media and direct mail pieces for the candidates.

This cadre of experienced campaign managers and workers along with the money and services that come with them give the candidates who receive a leader's support a tremendous advantage over candidates who are trying to put together and finance their own campaigns. It also creates a sense of obligation and loyalty on the part of the candidates who get leadership assistance. And, the leader's ability to raise money and direct campaigns also promotes loyalty and obligation toward the leader from all the members of the leader's legislative caucus, regardless of whether or not a member was or could be in a targeted race.

The challenger taking on an incumbent or going for an open seat in a politically competitive district rarely has any choice other than to accept the support of the legislative leader, even if he or she wants to be more independent. To be viable in these kinds of races requires huge sums of money. Faced with the task of raising $300,000 (or more), a candidate can take the money from the leader, or go in debt, or find 100 groups and individuals who will give her $3,000 each.

When incumbent legislators lose and open seats are captured by a new party, it almost always happens in a targeted race. In the 1994, 1996, and 1998 elections, a total of 19 incumbents lost and five open seats changed hands. In almost every case, the change occurred in a targeted race. During those three elections, no incumbent lost in the general election in a nontargeted race, and only one open seat flipped over to the other party in a nontargeted race. While incumbents almost always win in targeted races, the political mood of a particular election or the candidates in a particular contest can overcome the incumbent's natural advantage. In the 1994 Republican landslide that swept the country, 12 incumbent House Democrats lost in targeted races. In 1998, Mike Brown, an appointed Republican legislator, lost in the 63rd House District by 138 votes to Democratic challenger Jack Franks. Franks spent less than $120,000 and received less than $8,000 from the Democratic leader. Brown spent more than $180,000 and received more than $125,000 from the Republican leader. The outcome was heavily influenced by an ideological and geographical split among the district's Republicans and by the strength of the Democratic candidate's campaign.

One of the paradoxes of trying to reform campaign finance in Illinois is that the competition in legislative races in Illinois occurs in races that are dominated by money from the legislative leaders. In most cases, the leadership money does not make the race competitive. It only raises the overall cost of the election and blunts the advantage of the incumbent or majority party in the district. Hence the complexity of campaign finance reform: How do you facilitate competition without ceding extraordinary power to the legislative leaders, who then use that power to dominate the legislative process? Finding an answer that will pass the legislature and be signed by the governor is not an easy task.

The Gray Area of Nontargeted,
Competitive Legislative Campaigns

In between the world of targeted races and the world of uncontested races is a small class of races in which the losing candidate manages to raise enough money and gain enough visibility to push past the 40 percent mark without the help of a legislative leader. Money is important here as a threshold. During the 1994, 1996, and 1998 elections, losing candidates in nontargeted races who spent more than $50,000 got 40 percent or more of the vote slightly more than half the time. Losing candidates in nontargeted races who spent less than $50,000 got 40 percent or more of the vote in only one out of every 10 races. What we do not know is whether they become viable because they are able to raise some money, or they are able to raise some money because they are seen as viable. In most cases, the relationship is interactive. A few of these races may represent missed opportunities for the leaders.

In every election cycle, the leaders will shift money to a few races that look promising and away from races in which the candidate or the circumstances of the contest have been disappointing. These shifts will sometimes produce surprises, such as the win in 1992 by Democratic candidate Vickie Moseley in the 99th House District in Springfield. Running in a district drawn to favor a Republican candidate, Moseley was given little chance against Bill DeMarco, a well-known law enforcement officer. But the combination of her early campaign efforts and the weakness of her opponent's campaign caught the attention of House Speaker Madigan. He provided financial support and Springfield-based volunteers for her campaign during the last six weeks. Despite being outspent two-to-one, she easily won a race with a total cost of about $150,000. Two years later, she was defeated by Republican Raymond Poe in a very expensive targeted race in which the combined cost reached $346,000, more than double what was spent two years earlier.

The more normal fate for the losing candidate in these gray-area contests is that of Mike Goodman, who ran as the Democratic candidate in the 89th House District in 1996 and 1998. This is a district that strongly, but not overwhelmingly, favors a Republican candidate. In 1996, Goodman spent almost $40,000 and got 47 percent of the vote against incumbent Republican Jay Ackerman. In 1998, Goodman spent slightly more than $60,000 and got 43 percent of the vote against Keith Sommer, a nonincumbent Republican who spent more than $149,000. What would have happened if the House Democrats had targeted the race in 1996 or 1998? The House Republicans would certainly have matched the money and manpower of the Democrats. The spending on those races would have been much higher. And would the outcomes have been different? There is no way to tell. But strategically, the House Democrats clearly thought they had stronger needs in terms of protecting a seat they already held or a better chance to pick up a House seat elsewhere.

In almost every election cycle, a race involving an incumbent or an open seat will become much more competitive than either side anticipated. When that happens, either or both of the legislative leaders involved will usually (but not always) start putting money into the race. In 1998 in the 59th House District, Democrat Susan Garrett won an open seat with 54 percent of the vote in spite of being outspent $211,000 to $149,000 by Republican Christopher Stride. This is a district that has a very strong Republican-base vote. Stride received just less than $58,000 in support from the Republican leadership while Garrett received less than $5,000 from the Democratic leader. It just goes to show, as experienced as the legislative leaders are in targeting races, they are not perfect.

Money in Legislative Primary Races

For heavily Democratic areas, such as most of Chicago, and heavily Republican areas, such as DuPage County, the primary election is *the* election. The winner of the Democratic primary in most of Chicago's legislative districts easily will win the November general election, as will the winner of the Republican primaries in

DuPage County. Legislative leaders are actively involved in recruit-ing and assisting candidates in primary elections. When those pri-maries are contested, candidates recruited by the legislative leaders will receive financial support from the leaders' personal campaign committee rather than from a chamber political committee.

Primaries are usually less expensive, for several reasons, than gen-eral election contests. They involve fewer potential voters, the atten-tion level is lower, and partisan-oriented interest groups keep their money out of the race because they are likely to be happy with whichever candidate emerges as the winner. But, as in all other Illinois elections, spending in primaries has been increasing dramat-ically. In the current environment, primary spending tends to get heavy when there is an open seat in a one-party district, or when an incumbent in a one-party district receives a challenge based on a conflict over ideology or control of local politics.

There were two primary contests for open Senate seats in one-party districts in 1994 in which combined spending topped $300,000. In 1996, there was one open Senate primary in which spending exceeded $200,000, while in 1998 there were two. On the House side, combined spending exceeded $150,000 in two primary contests for open seats in 1994. In 1996, a primary contest for an open House seat topped the $200,000 combined spending mark, and two others racked up total costs of more than $150,000. In 1998, two more House primaries ran up more than $150,000 worth of total expenses.

If an incumbent faces an unexpected primary challenge, the indi-vidual leader becomes a critical source of money. Leaders often will back their candidates with transfers from their personal campaign accounts. And incumbents always can raise money from groups seeking access to power. Challengers, of course, have a harder time. During the 1994, 1996, and 1998 elections, a handful of conserva-tive candidates mounted serious challenges to moderate suburban Republican legislators. Some were financed by groups on the reli-gious right. In each case, incumbents won, and the leaders played key roles in providing their support. In 2000, only one Republican incumbent lost in the primary. That was in the 64th House District where Cal Skinner, Jr., a controversial conservative incumbent, lost by 10 percentage points to Rosemary Kurtz, a more moderate challenger, in a race in which each side spent more than $100,000.

In the 1998 and 2000 primaries, opponents sponsored by rival party ward organizations challenged a number of House Democratic legislators from Chicago. In the 2000 primary, five of those challenges were successful. And the spending was significant, averaging almost $100,000 per candidate. Incumbent legislators were able to call on interest groups and their legislative leaders to supplement local party money, while the challengers were financed almost exclusively by local party money. In the 4th House District, Edgar Lopez, the losing incumbent, spent more than $155,000. Of that, $40,000 came from the Illinois Education Association, $10,000 came from the Illinois State Medical Society, and more than $15,000 came from the speaker of the Illinois House. The winning challenger, Cynthia Soto, spent more than $191,000. Of that, more than $150,000 came from political committees, primarily from U.S. Congressman Louis Gutierrez. The Chicago Teachers Union gave $2,500 to each candidate, while the Illinois Trial Lawyers Association gave $3,500 to Soto and $1,500 to Lopez. The $347,000 spent by both candidates is a record for a House primary race. These kinds of spending patterns would not be possible without the permissiveness of the Illinois campaign finance law, which fosters a wide-open system that doesn't in any way restrict transfers from one political committee to another or impose contribution limits.

Interest Group Money and Contributions
from Individuals in Legislative Elections

As discussed in Chapter 3, at least half the private sector contributions that pour into elections come from people, groups, or corporate entities because they want access to power, not because they are concerned over the election fortunes of incumbent legislators or the legislative leaders. Most trade associations, professional associations, corporations, and unions do not contribute money to nonincumbents. Instead, they contribute money to leaders and to incumbent legislators because they already have power in the legislative process. Further, the groups give on a largely nonpartisan basis. If the Democrats are in power in the House, they will control the legislative process and have more incumbents. Interest groups contributing to House leaders and members will favor the Democrats for that reason. But a change in control of the House would cause money to shift toward the Republicans.

During the 1998 election cycle, candidates in targeted legislative races raised more than $20 million. About 60 percent of that money came as transfers from legislative leaders and other party committees. At the same time, candidates in nontargeted races raised more than $18 million. But that $18 million was raised almost entirely by incumbents, and only a small amount of that money came as transfers from legislative leaders or party committees. That means a lot of private money goes to incumbent legislators who do not have re-election concerns.

The fact that interest groups overwhelmingly favor incumbents when making campaign contributions gives legislative elections in Illinois a strong status quo bias. Nonincumbents need money more than incumbents, but incumbents have a much easier time raising money. The fact that interest groups give a very large portion of their contributions to leaders and give them on a nonpartisan basis also adds to the status quo bias. Groups concerned about access also will give more to the leaders who are in charge of each chamber. This also reinforces existing power relationships while adding to leadership power. As a result, groups who don't care strongly about elections end up providing the fuel for leaders to fund targeted races.

During the 1997-1998 election cycle, the following non-election-oriented groups each gave more than $150,000 to the Democratic legislative leaders and members *and* more than $150,000 to the Republican legislative leaders and members: the Associated Beer Distributors of Illinois, Ameritech, the Illinois Cable Television Association, Commonwealth Edison, Illinois Bankers Association, Illinois Hospital and HealthSystems Association, and Philip Morris Companies Inc.

While most interest groups are not directly interested in the outcome of elections, there is a relatively small, but very powerful group of associations, unions, corporations, and individuals who are intensely interested in who wins elections in Illinois. First, there is the small group of statewide associations who work elections directly as part of their overall lobbying strategy. These groups feel that the best way to ensure that they have friends in the legislature is to find a friend and help him or her get elected. These election-oriented interest groups provide money, services, and human resources to incumbents with difficult races and to challengers who are favorable to the group's policy positions. These groups give large amounts of money. They do direct mail pieces, make media buys, and staff telephone banks. Most of these groups also care which party controls the legislature. They believe that their policy interests will be affected if control of the legislature shifts from one party to the other. Groups with these kinds of partisan orientations also will contribute heavily to the legislative leaders of the party they favor. The major election-oriented groups are the American Federation of State, County and Municipal Employees (AFSCME); the Illinois Chamber of Commerce; the Illinois Education Association; the Illinois Federation of Teachers; the Illinois Manufacturers' Association; the Illinois State AFL - CIO; the Illinois State Medical Society; and the Illinois Trial Lawyers Association. Each of these groups contributed more than $50,000 to candidates in targeted legislative races and gave more than $50,000 to the legislative leaders.

The Illinois State Medical Society and the Illinois Trial Lawyers Association have battled over the issue of tort reform as it relates to medical malpractice for more than two decades. The leadership contributions of the Illinois State Medical Society are heavily slanted in favor of the two Republican leaders and Republican candidates, while the Illinois Trial Lawyers Association gives exclusively to the two Democratic leaders and Democratic candidates. Both groups are heavily involved in targeted races election cycle after election cycle. In the 1997-1998 election cycle, the Illinois State Medical Society gave more than $591,000 to the two Republican legislative leaders and more than $98,000 to Republican candidates in targeted legislative races. The Illinois Trial Lawyers Association gave more than $78,000 to the two Democratic legislative leaders and more than $168,000 to Democratic candidates in targeted legislative races.

Teacher unions are heavily involved in legislative elections, although the approaches of the two major groups are quite different. In the 1997-1998 election cycle, the Illinois Federation of Teachers (IFT), with which the Chicago Teachers Union is affiliated, gave more than $136,000 to the two Democratic legislative leaders and more than $361,000 to Democratic candidates in targeted legislative races. The federation gave only $2,000 to Republican legislative leaders and less than $5,000 to Republican candidates in targeted legislative races. In contrast, the Illinois Education Association (IEA) gave more than $229,000 to Democratic candidates and more than $197,000 to Republican candidates in targeted legislative races in the 1997-1998 election cycle. The association also gave more than $43,000 to Democratic leaders and more than $32,000 to Republican leaders. The bipartisan orientation of the Illinois Education Association stands in stark contrast to most groups that have a strong election orientation.

The IEA and the IFT are prime examples of how groups with money can have a significant impact on the funding of candidates in targeted legislative races. In the 1998 general election, the IEA gave $34,500 to one House candidate and more than $20,000 to six other House candidates. It gave $37,900 to one Senate candidate and more than $20,000 to three other Senate candidates. The IFT gave more than $20,000 to three House candidates and more than $20,000 to five Senate candidates. Combined IEA/IFT support of one Senate candidate was more than $63,000 and more than $49,000 for one House candidate. The two unions also spent more than $20,000 each supporting opposing candidates in two targeted House races and one targeted Senate race. As with leadership contributions, large interest group contributions in targeted races raise questions about the relationships and obligations that are being created.

While most election-oriented groups use their election activity and campaign contributions in conjunction with an access/face-to-face lobbying strategy to achieve their policy goals, there are exceptions. Personal PAC, a pro-choice group, gave the vast majority of its campaign contributions to candidates in targeted or competitive districts.

Very little of the more than $325,000 the PAC contributed during the 1997-1998 election cycle went to safe incumbents. None of it went to legislative leaders. Most groups that pursue an election strategy with campaign contributions also have broad legislative agendas that require them to build access to members of the state legislature.

In addition to those groups that actively work campaigns, there are interest groups and private corporations that are partisan but do not have the resources or the inclination to work campaigns. They contribute primarily to candidates from one party. They will contribute to candidates in targeted races and even to challengers in nontargeted races. Some will make large contributions to the leaders of the political party they support. But, overall most of their contributions are modest, less than $5,000. The primary distinction between these groups and the election-oriented groups cited above is that these groups do not work campaigns directly with mailings, polls, media buys, or human resources. Examples of highly partisan groups that gave more than $100,000 to the leaders and candidates of the Republican Party and less than $50,000 to the Democrats during the 1997-1998 election cycle are Caterpillar Corporation, Chamberlain Manufacturing, GTE Corporation, the Professional Independent Insurance Agents of Illinois, Ryan Holding Corporation of Illinois, and United Parcel Service. Similar examples of groups who support primarily Democratic leaders and candidates are Hotel Employees and Restaurant Employees International Union Tip Education Fund (TIP), the Service Employees International Union Illinois Council, Teamsters Drive Political Fund, United Auto Workers Illinois PAC, and the United Food and Commercial Workers Local 881.

In contrast to the access orientation of interest-group and corporation money, contributions from individuals are primarily election-oriented. In general, money from individuals goes to a specific candidate to help that candidate win an upcoming election. In the case of a few large donors, money goes to a legislative leader in support of the election of the leader's candidates for legislative seats. An example of such a financial angel on the Republican side is Stuart Levine, a prominent investor and businessman, who gave $117,500 to the two Republican legislative leaders during the 1997-1998 election cycle. Fred Eychaner, the president of the Newsweb Corporation, gave $100,000 to the two legislative leaders on the Democrat side.

While deep-pocketed individuals, associations, corporations, and unions that use campaign contributions to pursue an election strategy are few in number, their impact on elections and policy is very significant. Being able to use money to deal in access and elections gives them a tremendous advantage with both members of the General Assembly and the legislative leaders. With $1.9 million in contributions during the 1997-1998 election cycle, the Illinois Education Association is a dominant force in the legislature. The same is true of the Illinois State Medical Society with $1.45 million in campaign contributions. We will explore the way money directly influences policymaking in the next chapter. But it is obvious that who gets elected in the first place has a huge impact on what policy decisions are made.

Running for Statewide Office — Candidate-Centered Campaigns

We know less about the role of money in constitutional officer elections than we do about the role of money in legislative elections. There are only six statewide offices governed by Illinois campaign finance rules: governor, lieutenant governor, secretary of state, attorney general, treasurer, and comptroller. (The primary winners for governor and lieutenant governor run as a team in the general election.) The elections take place less frequently, every four years. While the statewide political forces care about all of the statewide offices, the news media care about only two, the governor and secretary of state. The majority of statewide private sector interests really care only about who is elected governor.

As noted earlier, the role of state and county political parties in primary or general election campaigns for statewide office has been declining since at least the election of Governor Dan Walker in 1972. In 1998, the governor, secretary of state, and comptroller races were open seats, while the attorney general and treasurer had

Republican incumbents. In the model of candidate-centered politics, the other candidates recruited themselves, built their own campaign organizations, raised their own money, and ran their own campaigns. The same pattern of every man or woman for himself or herself prevailed in the general election.

The difference in spending among the offices is dramatic. In 1998 the two candidates for governor spent more than $14 million in the general election and the two candidates for secretary of state spent $3.3 million. In contrast, the attorney general candidates spent $1.8 million, the comptroller candidates spent $1.8 million, and the treasurer candidates spent $1.1 million. By comparison, the two candidates in the most expensive state Senate race spent $1.4 million in the general election.

The cost of running for statewide office has been increasing dramatically. Except for one, every candidate who ran for statewide office in 1998 spent at least $1.3 million on winning the primary and running in the general election. The exception, Miriam Santos, was running under an ethical cloud involving fundraising abuses connected with her office as Chicago city treasurer, and she was running against a popular incumbent attorney general. Prior to 1998, candidates for comptroller and treasurer had never spent more than $1 million in the primary and general election. In 1998, all four candidates each spent more than $1.3 million. The $9.8 million George Ryan spent in the general election to win the governor's race was a record for a candidate for statewide office in Illinois.

While it takes a lot of money to get into the game and even more to win, money is still only a means to an end. Other factors can be substituted for money to generate political support. The winner in the Democratic gubernatorial primary was Glenn Poshard, a U.S. congressman from southern Illinois who had never run for statewide office. He spent $2.1 million. John Schmidt, another first-time candidate, spent $5.2 million and ran third. The candidate who ran second spent only $255,000. But he was Roland Burris, a former state comptroller and attorney general who had run for governor in 1994. He was also an African American with a strong voter base in Chicago in a four-candidate primary.

Compared to legislative candidates in targeted races, candidates for statewide office raise more money from individuals and interest groups and get less support from party sources. Only about 10 percent of the money raised by statewide candidates comes from party sources, while, as we've seen, candidates in targeted legislative races get more than 60 percent of their funds from party sources. On the other hand, only about 12 percent of the funds raised by legislative candidates in targeted races comes from individuals or as small contributions (under $150). Candidates for statewide office get 38 percent of their funds from individuals and small contributions. While interest groups and corporation money accounts for 25 percent of the money raised by legislative candidates in targeted races, typically 48 percent of the money raised by candidates for statewide office comes from interest groups and corporations.

Candidates for governor raise a significant portion of their money from a relatively small number of contributors. Because of the absence of limits on who can give or how much they can give, groups and corporations with money can have a significant impact on a campaign through very large campaign contributions.

In 1994, Governor Jim Edgar raised $20,000 or more from 36 contributors in his successful bid for re-election. Those contributors accounted for $1.37 million (or 13 percent) of the $10.8 million he raised. Four years later in 1998, 75 contributors each gave George Ryan $20,000 or more for his successful run for the Governor's Mansion. Those contributors accounted for $3.3 million (or 20 percent) of the $16 million he raised. The five largest interest-group contributors to Ryan's campaign were the Illinois Education Association ($273,000), the Illinois State Medical Society ($184,000), Illinois Manufacturers' Association ($124,000), the Illinois Cable Television Association ($88,000), and the Hotel Employees and Restaurant Employees International Union TIP Education Fund ($77,000).

On the Democratic side in 1998, in spite of Glenn Poshard's pledge not to take more than $5,000 from any interest group, a number of groups made large campaign expenditures on his behalf. The Illinois AFL-CIO spent more than $374,000 on television and radio ads on Poshard's behalf, while the Illinois Federation of

Teachers spent almost $75,000 in support of Poshard's campaign.

Self-funded campaigns for the state legislature are very rare. They are more frequent in campaigns for statewide office. In 1994, Al Hofeld, a successful trial lawyer, contributed or loaned more than $4.4 million of his own money to his unsuccessful campaign for attorney general. In 1994, the husband of Dawn Clark Netsch, the Democratic candidate for governor, loaned or contributed more than $1.34 million to her unsuccessful campaign. In 1998, John Schmidt, who finished third in the Democratic primary for governor, gave or loaned his own campaign more than $1.7 million. Al Salvi, the losing Republican candidate for secretary of state in 1998, gave or loaned his campaign more than $635,000. None of these cases resulted in anyone buying an election, but they do help raise the bar in terms of how much it costs to run a viable campaign for statewide office.

So, the cost and competition for statewide office continues to grow. While Illinois law allows unlimited contributions from interests groups, unions, corporations, and individuals, the high cost of running for statewide office means that no single source or interest dominates the process. But, the need to raise large sums of money to run statewide means that candidates without great personal wealth or the support of a strong party organization must develop relationships with those who have money to contribute. In this environment, both the appearance and the reality of these relationships have strong implications for the making of public policy and the administration of state government.

Money in Appellate and Supreme Court Elections

Illinoisans elect judges at the trial court level (circuit court judges), the appellate court level, and the Supreme Court level. Another class of judges, associate judges, who handle minor trial and administrative matters, are appointed by the circuit court judges. When an elective bench seat is open, candidates run for nomination in partisan primary elections with the winners facing off in the general election. Thus, in Illinois, judges are initially elected under partisan labels.

Once elected, circuit court judges serve six-year terms and appellate and Supreme Court justices serve 10-year terms. After an elected judge's first term has expired, he or she has the option of running for retention. In a retention election, the judge runs without an opponent and without a party label. The only question is whether or not the judge should be retained for another term.

Analyzing how the state's campaign finance system influences the judicial election process and possibly the judicial process itself is tricky. We know very little about judicial elections at any level. Contested elections occur on an irregular basis. Partisan political interest is usually local or regional rather than statewide. The news media and statewide private sector interests largely ignore judicial elections, even those for the Illinois Supreme Court.

But, on paper, the process seems straightforward enough. Supreme Court and appellate court judges run from one of five judicial districts. The First District is Cook County, which is strongly Democratic. Two Supreme Court justices and 24 appellate court judges are elected from the First District. The Second District is made up of counties to the west and north of Cook County and is strongly Republican. The Third District is made up of counties in north central Illinois, and the Fourth District is made up of counties in central Illinois. Both the Third and Fourth districts tend to vote Republican in partisan elections, but both are competitive. One Supreme Court justice and nine appellate court judges are elected from the Third District. One Supreme Court justice and six appellate court judges are elected from the Fourth District. The Fifth District is in deep southern Illinois and the metro-east area and is strongly Democratic. One Supreme Court justice and seven appellate court judges are elected from the Fifth District.

Because of the partisan geography of Illinois, judicial elections for both Supreme Court and appellate court positions almost never are competitive in the general election in the First, Second, and Fifth districts. Whoever wins the primary of the majority party also wins the general election. General election contests for appellate and Supreme Court seats are usually competitive in the Third and Fourth judicial districts. In 1998 the two winners of Democratic primary contests for appellate seats in the First District won easily in the general election. A race for an appellate court seat in the Fourth District was competitive that fall, as the Democratic candidate won with 54 percent of the vote in what many considered a mild upset. In 1996, Democratic primary winners for three appellate seats in the First District won without opposition in the fall. The same was true of the winner of the Republican primary for an appellate seat in the Fourth District, but the contest for an appellate seat in the Third District was very competitive in the general election, with the Democrat winning with 51 percent of the vote.

At the same time that there were three partisan elections for appellate court seats in 1998, there were also seven retention elections for sitting appellate court judges. Every sitting judge won easily. In 1996, there was only one sitting appellate court judge running for retention. He also won easily. Since 1975, no more than a handful of judges at any level have lost retention elections.

Prior to 2000, the last time Illinois had an election for a Supreme Court seat was in 1992. In 1990, the two Democratic candidates running for Supreme Court seats in the First District won easily, while the Republican candidate defeated the Democratic candidate by less than 3,000 votes for the Supreme Court seat from the Third District. In 1992, the Democratic candidates for a seat from the First District and the seat from the Fifth District won easily, while the Republican candidate for the seat from the Second District won without opposition.

In the 2000 primary, there was a very expensive primary for the Democratic nomination for a Supreme Court seat from the First District and a very expensive primary race for the Republican nomination for the Supreme Court seat from the Second District. As noted above, winning these primaries is traditionally tantamount to winning the seat. There was a competitive primary for the Republican nomination for the Supreme Court seat in the Third District, even though the winner of that contest was more likely to face a competitive race in November 2000. The same pattern took place at the appellate level, with a contested primary for the Democratic nomination for a seat from the First District and a contested primary for the Republican nomination for a seat from the

Second District. (Neither winner expected to face a serious contest that fall.) Both party nominations were strongly contested for the appellate seat open in the Third District, even though the general election in November was likely to be a competitive one.

What role does money play in judicial elections at the appellate level in Illinois? Because we know so little about the history of campaign contributions to judicial elections and their impact, the answers now can be only tentative. But, the trends from the last two elections are troubling.

Two facts are self-evident. First, money is not a factor in retention elections, which are largely ignored by voters and the news media. Second, money is not a factor in the general election in districts that lean heavily toward one party. In 1998, Michael Gallagher, a Democratic candidate for an appellate court seat in the First District, spent less than $17,000 and got 73 percent of the vote, while his Republican opponent, Sam Amirante, spent more than $104,000 and got 27 percent of the vote. Money is just not a major factor in these types of judicial elections.

The past two elections tell a different story for contested primary elections in one-party districts and general elections in competitive districts. It appears that these kinds of races are rapidly becoming more expensive. In 1998, the two candidates for an appellate court seat in the Fourth District spent a combined $272,000 in the general election. Sue Myerscough, the winning Democratic candidate, spent $133,000, while Thomas Appleton, the losing Republican candidate, spent $139,000. That was in addition to the $62,000 he spent to win the Republican primary. In the only appellate court race that was competitive in the 1996 general election, the two candidates spent a total of $126,000. No candidate spent more than $47,000 in any appellate court primary election in 1996. In 1998, the candidate who finished second in the Democratic primary for an appellate court seat in the First District spent $185,000. So, while the number of cases is small, the direction of the trend is toward more expensive judicial elections at the appellate court level.

The Myerscough-Appleton appellate court race illustrates two very different approaches to funding a campaign. Appleton raised

$213,000 in 1998. Of that, more than $118,000 came from loans or contributions from the candidate and his wife. More than $39,000 came from small (under $150), not-itemized contributions. The Sangamon County Republicans were his third-largest source of funds with more than $10,500 in contributions. Contributions from law firms and lawyers accounted for less than $8,000. Contributions from the candidate, small contributions, and contributions from a county political party accounted for more than $167,000 of the $214,000 he raised.

Myerscough raised $130,000 in 1998. Of that, $39,000 came from small (under $150), not-itemized contributions. The state Democratic Party contributed $33,000. Contributions from labor unions totaled more than $15,000, while contributions from law firms and lawyers were more than $13,000. Small contributions, the state Democratic Party, and interest groups accounted for more than $100,000 of the $130,000 she raised.

The 2000 primary races for Illinois Supreme Court seats show similar patterns of exploding costs and a heavy reliance on either interest groups or candidate loans and contributions. In the Democratic primary in the First District, the winning candidate, Thomas R. Fitzgerald, raised more than $690,000 of his total of $1,047,000 from interest groups. Lawyers and law firms accounted for more than $564,000 in contributions, businesses for more than $77,000, and labor unions for more than $43,000. Four law firms, Corboy and Demetrio; Clifford Law Offices; Motherway, Glenn and Napleton; and Powers, Rogers and Smith gave Fitzgerald a total of more than $159,000 among them. William Cousins, the candidate who ran second in the primary, raised almost half of his total of $242,000 from interest groups. Morton Zwick, who finished fourth, raised $1,063,000. Of that, $866,000 came from interest groups ($566,000 from businesses and $234,000 from lawyers and law firms).

In the Republican primary in the Second District, the winning candidate, Bob Thomas, raised $554,000. Of that, more than $409,000 came from interest groups. Lawyers and law firms gave $232,000 and businesses gave $176,000. Four law firms gave more than $120,000 among them. Bonnie Wheaton, who finished second, loaned or contributed $1.345 million to her campaign. She raised a total of $1,503,000. S. Louis Rathje, who finished third, raised slightly more than $1,059,000. Of that, $700,000 was self-financed in the form of contributions and loans. Another $267,000 came from interest groups ($158,000 from businesses and $103,000 from law firms and lawyers).

In the Republican Supreme Court primary in the Third District, the winning candidate was state Senator Carl Hawkinson. He used his legislative political committee to fund $210,000 of the $296,000 he raised with another $18,000 coming from the political committees of other legislators. His opponent, William Holdridge, raised $268,000, of which $107,000 came from law firms and lawyers and $30,000 from candidate contributions and loans.

Much like interest groups seeking access to the legislative process or the governor, some law firms gave to most of the candidates who were running, regardless of party or district. The Clifford Law Offices gave a total of $165,400 to six of the eight candidates running in the three contested Supreme Court primaries. Powers, Rogers and Smith gave $115,000 to seven of the eight candidates in the same primaries. Corboy and Demetrio gave $111,850 to five of the eight candidates. These contributions raise questions about the reasons behind them. When the Clifford law firm gives to all three candidates in one primary and two of the three candidates in another primary, and Powers, Rogers and Smith gives to all the candidates in two primaries and two of the three in a third, the clear intention is to establish a relationship with whomever wins rather than to back the "best" candidate.

Prior to the 2000 primaries, no candidate for an Illinois Supreme Court seat had raised more than $580,000 for the primary and general election periods combined. In 2000, four candidates raised more than $1 million for the primary period alone. The old record for combined spending by a field of candidates in a Supreme Court primary was $804,000 in 1992. The candidates in the Second Judicial District raised and spent more than $3 million.

Do the trends toward more expensive judicial elections and a greater role for interest group money cause concern? It's true that the minimum level of funding necessary to be viable keeps increasing. So, potential candidates will have to fund their own campaigns or solicit support from interest groups or party organizations. But that need for more money and the large role of interest groups in funding judicial elections raises serious questions about the perception and the reality of judicial independence.

Interest group money in judicial campaigns stirs concerns about the kinds of relationships that are being created and the kinds of campaigns being run. In partisan elections for the legislature or for statewide office, those giving money and the candidates taking it generally acknowledge that money gains access. Many interest groups endorse candidates and work campaigns because they want someone who is friendly toward their interests to be elected. The clear expectation is that those they have supported at least will be open to communication about policy issues and may even look out for the group's interests.

How the money in judicial elections gets spent is also a concern. With enough money, any candidate can hire consultants who will use polls, strategy, and campaign techniques to shape the candidate and the campaign in order to appeal to the voters in the election district. How do these concepts translate into the process of electing judges? Judicial ethics are supposed to keep judicial candidates from taking public positions on matters that may come before the court. Yet, the winning candidate in the Republican primary for the Supreme Court seat from the Second District put out a direct mail piece stressing his pro-life beliefs. And, before the end of the campaign, the abortion positions of all three candidates in the district had been widely publicized. The pro-choice group Personal PAC made more than $50,000 in expenditures on behalf of the losing candidates. The style and tone of the campaign for the Democratic primary in the First District was modern in every way, including television attack ads. The candidate who ran the negative ads paid a heavy price in negative publicity and finished fourth, but the differences between a judicial election and any other election in Illinois are growing smaller and smaller.

Expensive judicial elections funded by interest groups or wealthy candidates are troubling trends. Can only wealthy candidates or candidates who are willing to take money from special interests raise enough money to gain viability? Are candidates running for judicial office in order to advance policy agendas?

The appearance and the reality of fairness is the touchstone of the American judicial system. The ideal is that impartial judges will apply the law to the facts of a case and to the procedures of the judicial process. But, by making the process of selecting judges an elective one, we open the justice system up to modern election-style politics. And that process begets access-seeking contributors and candidates who must run on policy issues in order to win votes. In Illinois we have to ask if electing judges in the wide-open political environment doesn't seriously undermine the appearance of judicial impartiality, if not judicial impartiality itself.

Does Money Matter?

Money does matter in Illinois elections.

First, money is a barrier to entry into the political process for candidates. Each election cycle, it takes more money for nonincumbents to be visible, let alone viable. Each election cycle, it takes more money to win an open seat. And candidates must finance their own campaigns, raise money from interest groups and other private sources, or take money from a legislative leader or some other local or state elected public official. For many potential candidates, the "wealth primary" knocks them out of the running before they even start. Faced with the prospect of raising $150,000 for a House seat or $300,000 for a Senate seat or at least a million dollars for a run for statewide office, they quit before they begin.

Second, too much and too little money are barriers to competition. Money can be the great equalizer for the nonincumbent, but for most nonincumbents it is an unobtainable dream. The Illinois system allows incumbents to maximize their advantage over nonincumbents because money flows easily through the process with no limits. Groups who want access give to incumbents because they are in power. The rich get richer and the challengers scramble for the odd change.

113

Third, the Illinois campaign finance system allows interest groups with money to take maximum advantage of their resources to elect candidates and create relationships. These groups have much more freedom to use their money than in states with effective contribution limits. The natural advantage of groups with greater resources over groups with fewer resources is amplified in the Illinois system.

Fourth, the campaign finance system in Illinois allows legislative leaders and constitutional officers to amass unlimited sums of money from private sources. When the legislative leaders bring their resources to bear on a targeted legislative race, the importance of money is further amplified. What might have been a $200,000 or $300,000 House race can become an $850,000 race. What might have been a $500,000 Senate race can become a $1 million campaign. Being the best — and often the only — source of such large sums of money greatly enhances the power of legislative leaders.

Fifth, it now appears that the role money plays in legislative and statewide elections is rapidly becoming a core part of judicial elections for Illinois' appellate courts and the state Supreme Court. Given the openness of Illinois' campaign finance system, the importance of the decisions that these judges must make, and the basic nature of Illinois politics, this trend is not surprising. As troubling as the current system is for legislative and statewide constitutional office elections, the prospect of judicial elections taking place more and more in the same manner is even more troubling.

You Can't Sell a Car on Sunday

The Connection Between Money and Policy and (Sometimes) Scandal in Illinois

My daughter wanted to buy a car. I said I'd take her shopping on Saturday.

"Why not on Sunday?" she asked.

I told her that all the dealerships would be closed. Illinois state law prohibits automobile dealerships from operating on Sunday.

"Why would anyone pass such a dumb law?" she asked.

Why indeed?

Back in 1976, when their members decided that it would be nice to have one day a week off when they didn't have to worry about the competition of selling cars, the Illinois New Car and Truck Dealers Association pushed for a prohibition on Sunday sales. The bill became law, withstood a legal challenge, and has remained Illinois law ever since.

This "dumb law," as my daughter called it, passed and stands today for three reasons:

1. The law was backed by an organized group, in this case, the Illinois New Car and Truck Dealers Association.
2. The association employed a lobbying and campaign contribution strategy that opened legislative ears to its idea.
3. As a political group, people who might want to shop for a car on Sunday are unorganized and unrepresented.

A look at the association's structure and its contribution pattern will help illustrate why you're likely never to buy a car on Sunday in Illinois. The Illinois New Car and Truck Dealers Association is organized with its membership widely distributed throughout the state. The group is based in Springfield and has a full-time, paid staff that lobbies state government. And, the association has some money and spreads it around. Of the more than $209,000[1] in contributions it made in the 1997-1998 election cycle, more than $46,000 went to

---

[1] All dollar figures, unless otherwise noted, were generated from an Illinois campaign finance database created by the author. Support for the database was provided by The Joyce Foundation and the Institute for Public Affairs at the University of Illinois at Springfield. The database contains receipt and expenditure records beginning with January 1, 1993, and is updated every six months. As of August 2000, the database contained more than 400,000 records from more than 600 candidates for legislative and statewide offices.

the legislative leaders and more than $35,000 went to George Ryan, the successful candidate for governor. Besides the four top legislative leaders, there are 173 other members of the General Assembly. In the 1997-1998 election cycle, the Illinois New Car and Truck Dealers Association donated to 139 of them. Between 1993 and 1999, the association contributed more than $714,000 to incumbents and candidates for legislative and statewide office. The association consistently ranks among the top 30 contributors to Illinois politicians. The four legislative leaders took between $20,000 and $60,000 each from the Illinois New Car and Truck Dealers Association between 1993 and 1999.

So, does the longevity of the Sunday auto sales law prove that money buys policy in Illinois?

No. The Illinois New Car and Truck Dealers Association's biggest contribution to a single legislative leader was $11,000 in the 1997-1998 election cycle. Only three legislators received more than $2,000 during those two years, with $4,000 being the largest total contribution to a rank-and-file legislator. No votes are being bought and sold in Springfield at those prices.

But does money help?

Certainly. Money is a resource that groups use in gaining access and influence in Illinois politics.

The other advantage a group like the Illinois New Car and Truck Dealers Association has is the disorganization of its opposition. The people who are disadvantaged by the law and are in a position to benefit from its repeal are potential car buyers. If you are currently trying to buy a car, you probably won't want to wait for the legislature to change the law so you could shop on Sunday. If you don't think you will be buying a car in the immediate future, you don't have a strong reason to support a repeal of the Sunday ban. Only those who think they will be car shopping within the next year or two even marginally care about changing this law. Clearly, this is a group that is difficult to identify, much less organize.

A legislator who wanted to introduce a bill to repeal the Sunday car buying ban could count on the general support of consumer groups with large agendas, but that would be about it. A bill to repeal this law would be one of those measures that everyone is for in principle, but somehow gets lost along the way with the "help" of a committee chairman or legislative leader who is friendly with the organized opposition group. At a minimum, the Illinois New Car and Truck Dealers Association's contributions, in combination with its full-time lobbying presence and grassroots lobbying activities, provide it with extensive access and goodwill with the legislature. Passing a bill to allow Sunday car sales against the strong opposition of the Illinois New Car and Truck Dealers Association would be a very difficult task.

While legislators and governors like to talk about representing the unorganized and the disaffected, the reality is quite different. One of the truths of the political world is that organized interests usually prevail over unorganized interests, particularly if the organized interests have money to make campaign contributions.

Illinois is different from most states because the wide-open system of campaign finance allows groups with money to contribute to make maximum use of that resource. If Illinois had contribution limits and prohibitions on direct corporate donations, it would be more difficult for the New Car and Truck Dealers Association to move money into the system. Contribution limits also would place a ceiling on what leaders or members could ask from interest groups. Limits would not level the playing field, but they would lessen the advantage that groups with money have over groups without money.

Would contribution limits have prevented the ban from passing in the first place? Probably not.

Would limits make it more likely that the law would someday be changed? Without a doubt.

Limits on the role of money in politics will not eliminate the advantage in the process that organized groups that make large campaign contributions enjoy, but the continued absence of limits will make that advantage even greater.

The case of the ban on Sunday car sales is a fairly benign one. In this chapter, we'll take a look at several more recent and more egregious cases in which the largely unchecked flow of contributions to legislators — in particular to the legislative leaders — appears to have influenced public policy. Between the fall of 1997 and the spring of 1999, legislation favorable to the state's wine and spirits industry, the electric utility companies, and the gambling industry passed the legislature in the wake of those interest groups' infusing the campaign finance system with large amounts of cash, both in the form of contributions to legislative campaigns and the fees paid to high-powered lobbyists. In a more modest example, the payday loan industry played the game in reverse, by using its organization and resources to kill (at least temporarily) legislation that it deemed detrimental to its interests.

The wide-open system of campaign finance and the concentration of power in the state's legislative leaders and the governor creates an atmosphere in which well-heeled special interests have a huge advantage when it comes to influencing the General Assembly to enact what my daughter would call "dumb laws." Dumb laws are, of course, in the eyes of the beholder, and there is no law against passing a dumb law. But this system also has opened the government up to scandal. In this chapter we'll also take a look at how Illinois' unregulated campaign finance system contributed to public corruption in the awarding of a state contract and the issuing of commercial driver's licenses.

Campaign finance is not just about elections. It has real consequences for the policies that state government adopts and the ethical and moral climate in which it conducts its business. The impact can be as pervasive as the cost of electricity to homeowners, as obscure as the "closed" sign on the door of an auto dealership, or as dramatic as the root causes of the next widely publicized political scandal. How Illinois chooses to deal with the role of money in politics makes a difference in the everyday lives of citizens.

Money, Legislative Leaders, and Public Policy

The real danger for distortion and bias in public policy occurs when unrepresented or underrepresented interests face off against well-organized, well-funded interests. When one side is organized and well-funded and the other side is unorganized, the policy result is usually one-sided, as is the case with Sunday auto sales. The record of the General Assembly in 1999 in dealing with gambling expansion, liquor distributor contracts, and payday loan industry regulation suggests that the current system gives narrow interests with money a huge advantage over unorganized interests. Because part of that dynamic is the result of the role that campaign contributions play in maintaining the power of the legislative leaders, let's take a moment to review the breadth and depth of the power of the legislative leaders.

As explained in Chapter 4, political parties are alive and well in the Illinois General Assembly. But these are not the traditional Republican and Democratic parties. Rather, the parties in control of the Illinois General Assembly at the turn of the century are the House Speaker Michael Madigan Party, the Senate President James "Pate" Philip Party, the House Minority Leader Lee Daniels Party, and the Senate Minority Leader Emil Jones Party. These legislative leaders perform all of the traditional functions of political parties. They recruit the candidates, raise the funds, and run the campaigns. They also set the legislative agenda and consistently deliver the votes of their members on important roll calls. And they do all of this in a manner about which legislative leaders at the national level can only dream.

These leaders, often called the "Four Tops," have been entrenched in their positions. In fact, the group's most junior member, Jones, has been the Senate Democratic leader since 1993. The other three were already legislative leaders by 1984. Having the same leaders for even a decade is almost unprecedented in state legislatures in the modern era. Yet the long tenure or the political skills of the leaders does not explain why they are so powerful or why their power has steadily increased.

As we've seen in Chapter 4, one of the secrets to the power that legislative leaders hold their ability to raise millions in campaign contributions and direct the money to targeted legislative races. But the leaders also control the legislative staff and the formal procedures of the legislative process. The leaders often use a combination of human and financial resources to keep their members in line when it comes to voting on controversial issues.

When the General Assembly is in session, committee staff provides information on bills and amendments and support in drafting
and shaping legislation. But the legislative members or even the
committee chairmen do not hire those staff people. All the partisan
staff who do the substantive and appropriation committee work are
part of four centralized staffs, each controlled by one of the legislative leaders. The committee chairmen and minority spokesmen are
appointed by the leaders and work with people assigned from the
leaders' staffs. Call up a Democratic staff person who has responsibility for the House Transportation Committee or does the budget
analysis for mental health agencies for one of the House appropriation committees, and she will answer the phone, "Speaker Madigan's
staff." Ultimate control over staff rests, not with individual members
or even committee chairmen, but with the legislative leaders. In
addition, leadership staff members often provide support for the
rank-and-file members who are more political in nature. They do
the press releases, write the newsletters, organize district activities,
and provide information on legislation directly to members. These
resources are directed at all members, but the legislators perceived as
potential targets need and receive the most support. At election
time, some staffers — at the direction of the chamber leaders — will
leave the state payroll in the summer and fall to work full-time on
campaigns in targeted districts. Professional House and Senate
staffers are the ones who organize and run the campaigns.

A legislator who disagrees with her leader on an important bill
runs the risk of losing campaign contributions from the leader's
campaign account and the staff needed to mount a successful re-
election. An incumbent in a district that has been targeted in the
past or might be targeted in the future by the other side is well aware
that, come the next election, he or she may need all the resources the
legislative leader can bring. The individual members take very seriously the "suggestions" and "urging" that come from the legislative
leaders during the course of a legislative session.

The other source of power leaders have over their rank-and-file
underlings is their control of the legislative process itself. When the
legislature convenes in Springfield, the leaders have a monopoly not

only over staff but also over formal power to control the legislative agenda and determine most of the outcomes.

The controversy surrounding House passage of a bill sought by the cable television industry during the 1997 fall veto session illustrates the problems that can arise for individual members in this highly concentrated power structure. It also highlights the advantage that the top contributors enjoy in the legislative process in Illinois. In that veto session, a bill was introduced that would have pre-empted consumers' abilities to mount class action lawsuits against cable television companies over the way the companies were applying late charges to customers with past-due bills. The bill came up for a vote on the House floor after being moved out of committee earlier in the day. It was presented to the members of the House as a consumer-oriented, noncontroversial bill. It passed with 78 votes, more than enough to make the bill effective immediately. Afterward, negative press accounts of the potential impact of the bill combined with the public opposition of Illinois Attorney General Jim Ryan created a firestorm of criticism and finger pointing, which resulted in the Senate sponsor tabling the bill when the legislature came back a week later.

Much of the media attention focused on cable industry campaign contributions to the legislative leaders and individual members. The decade of the '90s was a time of explosive growth in the cable industry. With that growth came increasing government scrutiny and efforts at regulation. In response, campaign contributions from the cable industry increased steadily throughout the decade. In just three election cycles, the industry increased its contributions threefold from $148,000 in the 1993-1994 election cycle, to $325,000 in the 1995-1996 election cycle, to $483,000 in the 1997-1998 election cycle. The cable industry made a major commitment during the decade to becoming more effective in the legislative process, and campaign contributions were a key part of that effort.

The power structure of the legislature made the giving strategy easy. During the 1997-1998 election cycle, House Republican Leader Daniels raked in $70,000 from the Illinois Cable Television Association, while House Speaker Madigan got $42,000. In addition, the State Democratic Party, of which Madigan was chair, took in more than $18,000. Senate President Philip got $57,000, while Senate Democratic Leader Jones received $30,000. In total, the legislative leaders received $199,000 from the cable industry. In addition, individual legislators received more than $168,000 in cable industry contributions during the 1997-1998 election cycle, and soon-to-be-elected Governor Ryan took in more than $88,000.

New legislation is not considered and brought up for a vote in the veto session without the approval of the legislative leaders. And it is perhaps unfair to suggest that the cable bill made it on the agenda solely because the industry contributed so heavily. But, the fact that the bill was brought up for a vote in an accelerated manner speaks to the influence of the cable industry and its relationship to the legislative leaders.

In addition to being a classic example of the access to the process enjoyed by top contributors, the treatment of the cable bill also illustrates the impact that the dominant control of the leaders has on the nature of the legislative process. The comments of rank-and-file legislators as reported in the press focused on the role of the sponsor, the leaders, and the legislative staff in moving the bill (Pearson 1997). Members complained that they did not know what was in the bill, had not seen any staff analysis of the bill, and voted on the basis of the floor presentations made by the sponsor and other supporters of the bill. They also complained that, while no one informed them of the implications of what they were voting on, members who were potential targets in the next election received a heads up from somewhere and either voted against the bill or did not vote. The implication is that individual members had to depend on leadership staff and that the leaders did not take care of all members equally.

The Relationship Between Campaign Contributions, "Dumb Laws," and Corporate Welfare

The power of the legislative leaders over the process means that almost every group that makes campaign contributions gives a significant portion of its contributions to the leaders, regardless of the nature of the issues or whether its concerns are partisan or regional. Because the leaders can never be sure how much is enough money for the next set of political campaigns, they exert great pressure on interest groups and corporations to contribute. Because these groups and corporations want to be important players in the process, or, at a minimum, have access to the leaders, they continue to contribute more each election cycle. Control in the capital enhances control in elections and control in elections enhances control in the capital. It's a circle that could turn upon itself forever.

In this context, no incentives exist for the leaders to share their power with individual members or to alter the campaign finance system they have created. The individual legislative members become less independent, less influential, and the Four Tops stay on top. Limiting the role of money in the process, particularly as it relates to the power of the legislative leaders, would go a long way toward opening up the process and empowering individual members of the legislature.

In the absence of these reforms, the influence of big-time contributors appears to be strengthening. While no illegal contributions-for-legislation *quid pro quo* is in evidence in the legislative process, a spate of legislation extremely favorable to organized and well-financed special interests has recently passed through the General Assembly. For the next few pages, we'll examine the players and the outcomes involved in these measures. These cases will show that Illinois' no-holds-barred campaign finance system invites protectionist legislation and corporate welfare. If the people of Illinois are against laws like these, then one way to curb them is to enact campaign finance reform.

The Wine and Spirits Fair Dealing Act:
Liquor Distributors Distribute Money and Clout

On May 21, 1999, Governor George Ryan signed the Wine and Spirits Industry Fair Dealing Act into law. The new law prohibits liquor manufacturers with existing contracts with Illinois liquor distributors from canceling or changing those contracts unless the manufacturer makes a showing of "good cause" before the Illinois

Liquor Control Commission. The law was designed primarily to protect the financial interests of one company: Judge & Dolph, Ltd., a Chicago-based subsidiary of the Wirtz Corporation. The legislation was intended as protection in Illinois against problems that Wirtz-owned liquor distributorships had with liquor manufacturers in Nevada.

William Wirtz heads the Wirtz Corporation. He is also owner of the Chicago Blackhawks and a major figure in Chicago sports and business. The story of the Wine and Spirits Industry Fair Dealing Act is a classic example of the ease with which big money flows into the political process in Illinois and the direct and indirect ways big money shapes the outcomes of public policy.

When William Wirtz decided to seek help from the state for his liquor distribution business in 1998, he was not a stranger in Springfield, particularly to the legislative leaders in the House. Campaign contributions buy access. Individuals, corporations, and groups with money often will donate even though there are no pressing issues that affect the giver. In November 1994, a Nevada liquor distributorship owned by the Wirtz Corporation gave House Democratic Leader Michael Madigan a $15,000 contribution. The House Republicans won a majority in the election later that month, and in December, a Minnesota liquor distributorship owned by the Wirtz Corporation gave House Republican Leader Lee Daniels a $6,250 contribution. The Wirtz Corporation also gave Governor Jim Edgar a total of $5,000 in 1993 and 1994. The House Democrats regained control of the House in 1996. On November 5, 1996, a Texas-based liquor distributorship owned by the Wirtz Corporation gave the House Democratic chamber committee $20,000. That same day, a Wisconsin-based liquor distributorship owned by (you guessed it) the Wirtz Corporation gave the House Republican chamber committee a $20,000 contribution. Judge & Dolph also made a $1,000 contribution to Governor Edgar in 1996. In most state and in federal elections, direct corporate contributions to candidates are illegal, but not in Illinois. Here, they are an investment in the future, goodwill against a time when the interests of the giver are at stake.

While legislation creating the Wine and Spirits Industry Fair Dealing Act was formally introduced in the legislature in November of 1998, the campaign on its behalf had really begun almost a year earlier. The battle for influence proceeded on three money-driven fronts:

1. Campaign contributions from a political action committee.
2. Campaign contributions from the Wirtz Corporation.
3. The use of professional lobbyists.

In December 1997, the IWAPAC filed documents with the State Board of Elections as a political committee. The IWAPAC is the political arm of the Wine and Spirits Distributors of Illinois (WSDI). Under Illinois law the IWAPAC does not have to explain what the letters IWA stand for in its name, and citizens seeing IWAPAC on disclosure documents might not immediately recognize that these are liquor-related donations. Initial funding for the IWAPAC came from contributions from individual liquor distributors, including Judge & Dolph. In the second half of 1998, the funding for IWAPAC was changed to lump-sum transfers from the WSDI. The WSDI is not registered as a political committee and does not, therefore, file disclosure reports with the State Board of Elections. This, in turn, makes it impossible to tell who is funding the IWAPAC and in what amounts.

The IWAPAC hit the ground giving. In 1998, it handed out more than $123,000 to legislators and the candidate who would be elected governor in the fall election. A total of $15,000 went to House Speaker Madigan, $21,650 to House Republican Leader Daniels, $19,700 to Senate President Philip, and $7,500 to Senate Democratic Leader Jones. That's a total of $63,850 to the four legislative leaders. The IWAPAC also gave $4,300 to gubernatorial candidate George Ryan and more than $55,000 to individual legislators.

In addition to working through the IWAPAC in 1998, the Wirtz Corporation was giving money directly to Illinois political leaders. On May 11, 1998, five out-of-state liquor distributorships owned by the Wirtz Corporation each contributed $10,000 to the Republican candidate for governor, Secretary of State George Ryan. In all, Ryan received $50,250 directly from corporate interests controlled by the

127

Wirtz Corporation plus an individual contribution of $1,000 from William Wirtz. Between September 15 and October 13, 1998, liquor distributorships controlled by the Wirtz Corporation gave $70,000 to the four legislative leaders with all but $10,000 coming from out-of-state companies. House Speaker Madigan received $25,000, as did House Republican Leader Daniels, while Senate President Philip and Senate Democratic Leader Jones each received $10,000. For 1998, the combined contributions to the four legislative leaders and the governor-elect from companies owned by the Wirtz Corporation and the IWAPAC was more than $193,000. As noted above, individual legislators also received more than $55,000 in contributions from the IWAPAC. All of this money was contributed before the wine and spirits bill was introduced in November.

In addition to making direct contributions, groups, corporations, and individuals with money can hire lobbyists to represent their interests before the legislature and the governor. In 1998, a number of Wirtz Corporation employees were registered lobbyists in Springfield. At that time, the company also had a small number of contract lobbying firms and individual lobbyists on retainer. But by the time the Wine and Spirits Industry Fair Dealing Act passed the legislature in 1999, the number of contract lobbying firms and individual lobbyists employed by the Wirtz Corporation had grown to 23. Most notable were former Republican Governor James Thompson of the Winston and Strawn law firm, former Democratic Senate President Philip Rock, and a number of people connected to prominent Chicago law firms.

Contract lobbyists are hired because they know the process, know the people in state government, and have access and credibility with the governor, the legislative leaders, or the key members of the General Assembly. Lobbyists build relationships and expertise over time. This type of representation gives a corporation a huge advantage over groups that can't afford (or don't realize they need) experienced, Springfield-based people to represent them.

The top contract lobbyists or lobbying firms in Springfield do not come cheap. In Illinois, fee arrangements do not have to be disclosed. (They do in some states.) But typically, the fee for a single project at the Wine and Spirits Industry Fair Dealing Act-level will run five or six figures. Lobbyists' clients pay for the access and good-will that the lobbyist has earned over time.

How did the lobbyists get that access?

In part, by making campaign contributions. This process is not money laundering in which client money goes to a lobbyist with the understanding that it will be passed on to a specific politician. These are general contributions made in the name of the lobbyist or lob-bying firm. But, of course, lobbyists pass those costs on to clients when they create their pricing structures. (Notice, however, that con-tributions are not the primary source of the influence that contract lobbyists and lobbying firms have in the process. Former Governor Jim Thompson's value as a lobbyist does not rest on the more than $50,000 in contributions made by his political committee, Citizens for Thompson, between 1997 and 1999. But money is part of the package.) The lobbying firms and lobbyists the Wirtz Corporation employed gave more than $360,000 to legislative leaders, legislators, and constitutional officers in the 1997-1998 election cycle.

In 1999, both before and after the bill became law, the IWAPAC contributed an additional $103,000, with $11,000 going to Governor Ryan, $31,000 to the four legislative leaders, and $61,000 to individual legislators. (But the required campaign finance records show that the Wirtz Corporation itself contributed less than $5,000 in 1999.) During 1998 and 1999, total contributions from corpora-tions controlled by the Wirtz Corporation and from the IWAPAC were more than $357,000. Governor Ryan received more than $77,000. House Republican Leader Daniels got $55,000. House Speaker Madigan took in $52,000, and Senate President Philip and Senate Democratic Leader Jones received $30,000 each. Contributions to individual legislators totaled more than $123,000.

The Wirtz interests were successful from the beginning in charac-terizing the conflict as one between an Illinois business and big international companies. In contrast to the campaign contributions from the Wirtz side, the primary corporations involved in the dis-pute against Wirtz contributed almost nothing to state-level Illinois politicians during 1998 or 1999. They did hire a prominent contract-lobbying firm to represent them. The liquor manufacturers' strategy was largely one of framing the issue as a protectionist, anti-competitive measure that was bad public policy.

The Wine and Spirits Industry Fair Dealing Act passed the House in the fall of 1998 during the veto session, but stalled in the Senate. The Wirtz group started over in the spring of 1999. In spite of strong editorial opinion against the bill, it passed both the House and the Senate by large margins and was signed into law at the end of the spring session. While the liquor manufacturers probably won the policy debate, the Wirtz Corporation won the lobbying battle, and the bill became law.

The next arena is the courts. In January 2000, a U.S. District Court granted an injunction to stop the law's implementation. The suit arose when Kendall-Jackson Wine Estates tried to fire its Illinois distributor, which happened to be Judge & Dolph, Ltd. The judge who granted the injunction agreed with editorial opinion against the law and said it amounted to economic protectionism (Hammett 2000).

Regardless of whether it ultimately stands or falls, the Wirtz bill did become state law. Did the Wirtz Corporation buy that law?

In terms of a straight *quid pro quo*, the answer is no. But the company did sell the new law to the legislature and the governor with the help of campaign contributions and high-priced contract lobbyists.

As a prominent Illinois businessman, would Wirtz have been able to get the attention of the legislative leaders and the governor without making more than $300,000 in contributions and hiring 23 contract lobbyists?

Probably.

Would the legislation have been considered in the veto session at the end of the two-year legislative session?

Probably not.

Did Wirtz's advantage in campaign contributions and the lobbying activity make it much more difficult for the opponents to make their case with the legislative leaders and the governor?

Certainly.

Would limits on the role of money in Illinois politics produce a different outcome?

Probably, if the result were a less leadership-dominated, more open process with more independent members. But, as with all political reforms, that is a big *if*.

Interest groups, corporations, and individuals with narrow issues and legislative access and skill — or the money to purchase access and skill — will flourish in a system in which power is concentrated in the hands of a few leaders and the campaign finance process is wide open. The Wine and Spirits Industry Fair Dealing Act is not the kind of issue that a legislator is likely to feature in a constituent newsletter or a campaign ad. Very few legislators and even fewer citizens understood or cared about it as it moved through the legislature. But the legislative leaders and the governor did.

Turning Up the Juice –
The Power Companies and Electric Deregulation

The power companies knew that electric deregulation would be a fact of life long before the passage of a deregulation bill in the fall of 1997. It had happened to the telephone and airline industries, and many of the state's large corporations were pushing for the idea. So the state's utility companies resigned themselves to the fact that they would soon lose their monopolies in their service areas and be forced to allow competing companies to sell power to "their" customers.

But, deregulation is an extremely complex and important issue with broadly ranging implications for power producers and distributors, large and small businesses, and residential consumers. The initial law was passed in 1997, was modified in 1999, and its long-term impact is still up for debate. But some facts are not in dispute.

The potential impact of electric deregulation in Illinois was greatest for two power companies: Commonwealth Edison, known as ComEd (a subsidiary of Unicom) and Illinois Power (whose parent company is Illinova). In comparison to other power companies in the state, Commonwealth Edison and Illinois Power had higher rates, so the prospect of deregulation and price competition was particularly troubling for them. Both companies had huge capital investments in nuclear facilities, and if deregulation forced them to lower their rates to stay competitive, the companies might not be able to recover the cost of those plants. In technical terms, this is an issue of stranded costs.

Rather than trying to stop deregulation itself, the issue for ComEd and Illinois Power became a question of implementing deregulation in a way that allowed them to compete for customers and recover the costs of investments they made in the era of regulation. The potential impact on the stockholders of these companies was enormous: ComEd had an estimated $4.4 billion of stranded costs, and Illinois Power had $682 million (Ekert 1997). Of course, the method of deregulation was not up to the industry itself but up to the General Assembly. One of the responses the companies made to this environment of uncertainty was to dramatically increase their campaign contributions.

During the 1993-1994 election cycle, Commonwealth Edison contributed $136,000 to legislators and constitutional officers. In the 1995-1996 cycle, the total jumped to $256,000, and in the 1997-1998 cycle it jumped again to $406,000. Contributions from Illinois Power and Illinova rose from $108,000 in the 1993-1994 election cycle to $187,000 in the 1995-1996 cycle to $388,000 for the 1997-1998 cycle. Neither company ranked as one of the top 20 contributors for the 1993-1994 election cycle. For the 1997-1998 cycle, Commonwealth Edison ranked thirteenth and Illinois Power came in fourteenth.

As would be expected from the way that leadership dominates the legislative process in Illinois, a large portion of the contributions from Commonwealth Edison and Illinois Power went to the legislative leaders. In the 1997-1998 election cycle, more than $190,000 of Commonwealth Edison's contributions went to the legislative leaders. House Republican Leader Daniels received almost $52,000, while House Speaker Madigan took in more than $35,000. Senate President Philip got almost $51,000. Senate Democratic Leader Jones received $42,000. Illinois Power gave more than $160,000 in contributions to the legislative leaders in the 1997-1998 cycle. House Republican Leader Daniels got more than $58,000; House Speaker Madigan got $13,000; Senate President Philip took in more than $55,000; and Democratic Leader Jones received $48,000. In total, ComEd and

Illinois Power gave the two Republican leaders more than $100,000 each during the session the deregulation was approved. At the same time, the two utility companies gave Senate Democratic Leader Jones $90,000 and House Speaker Madigan $48,000.

At least two electric deregulation plans — one backed by ComEd and Illinois Power and the other backed by interests such as the Illinois Manufacturers' Association — got onto the legislative agenda in 1997. A plan more favorable to ComEd's and Illinois Power's interests passed the House but was nixed in the Senate, in favor of a business interest-backed measure that left the stranded costs of the two utility giants more exposed (Man 1997). Clearly, if deregulation was to occur, a compromise would have to be hammered out.

That compromise legislation, passed at the end of 1997, opened the industry up to deregulation, but only for businesses buying electricity. Residential customers aren't allowed to shop for the best rates until 2002. Also, until 2006, all customers who switch power companies are subject to a "transition fee," which would presumably help the larger utilities recover some stranded costs, even if their customers jump to a company that offers them lower electric rates (*Illinois Issues* 1997). Whatever the overall merits of the final electric deregulation bill, on the issues of stranded costs and a phase-in of residential customer choice, the interests of Commonwealth Edison and Illinois Power were protected. In the three years prior to and the year following the decision, contributions from these two power companies to the legislature — particularly to the legislative leaders — increased dramatically.

What does this prove, if anything?

Did these companies buy a favorable policy?

Certainly not in the sense of a direct *quid pro quo*. Contributions were only part of the lobbying effort that took place. Having full-time lobbyists and policy expertise is critical, particularly with a highly complex and technical set of issues like those involved with electric deregulation.

Was there a relationship between the way the legislation was shaped and these contributions?

Of course. Even if these contributions were only buying access, the result was an increased advantage that these companies enjoyed over largely unorganized consumer interests who do not contribute to legislative leaders and legislators. (Notice that business interests who did organize and contribute to legislative leaders were the first in line when it came to being granted the ability to choose their own electric companies.) The bottom line is this: It is not *impossible* for legislative leaders to say "no" to interest groups who donate hundreds of thousands of dollars, but the contributions make it much more difficult.

Beyond the specific policy outcome, the electric deregulation battle again shows how open the Illinois system is and how easy it is to move huge amounts of money into the process as quickly as an issue heats up. Limits on the role of money in the Illinois process would change significantly the dynamics of how we make public policy. Even generous limits of $5,000 per election would have capped each company's contribution to a leader at $10,000 per two-year election cycle. If the four legislative leaders had received a total of $80,000 from the two power companies instead of $350,000, the policy debate would have been more open. Even if the policy outcome were the same, its legitimacy in the eyes of the public, the news media, and the participants would have been enhanced.

Easy Money: Lobbying for Payday and Title Loan Companies

For many special interests the most favorable laws are the ones that don't get passed. This was the case for the payday loan industry in the spring of 2000.

Illinois has seen a marked increase in companies that make small loans at very high interest rates. Banking deregulation and consolidation in the late 1990s severely limited the availability of consumer loans of less than $1,000. In response, a new industry has grown to fill the need. Typically, payday loan borrowers give lenders a postdated check for the loan amount plus a fee. When the loan comes due, the loan company cashes the check and keeps the fee. If borrowers can't make good on their check, they often have the option of rolling the loans over (and incurring more fees). Title loan companies accept the title to the borrower's car as collateral for a short-term loan. If the borrower cannot pay the loan, he or she has the option of rolling the loan over or forfeiting title to the car. The way these companies operate has become very controversial. Because Illinois state law does not limit their interest rates, annual rates of 250 percent to 500 percent are common. Concerns have also been raised about aggressive, deceptive marketing.

Nineteen states had banned payday loan business as of August 2000 (Keith 2000). Legislatures in other states have adopted laws limiting the rates these companies can charge and regulating their business practices. Illinois has lagged behind in this area. An attempt to regulate the industry through legislation during the spring 2000 legislative session provides another illustration of the role that money can play in the Illinois lawmaking process. It also highlights the need for more frequent reporting of campaign contributions than the current system, which only requires comprehensive reports every six months.

Prior to 1999, the small loan industry in Illinois was unorganized, without a full-time lobbyist or a political action committee to make campaign contributions. Bills were introduced in the House and Senate in 1999 to regulate the industry and cap the interest rates. Faced with the prospect of legislation they viewed as harmful, individual companies banded together to form the Illinois Small Loan Association (ISLA). Given the negative public image of the industry, a public relations campaign to recast these loan companies as friends of the disadvantaged was not a strategic option. But in Illinois there are other options.

The loan association first secured representation from a prominent contract lobbyist. Then, in November 1999, the Illinois Small Loan Association registered as a political committee with the State Board of Elections. According to its 1999 semi-annual report and its 2000 primary pre-election report, ISLA raised more than $80,000 from its members between November 15, 1999, and February 20, 2000. On February 1, it gave $10,000 each to campaign committees controlled by the four legislative leaders. On February 25, Senate President Philip's political committee reported receiving an additional $10,000 from ISLA. In all, ISLA gave more than $80,000 to legislators and legislative leaders in the spring of 2000. The spring legislative session adjourned that April with a Senate regulatory bill dead and a House bill stuck in committee.

This is not to say that the industry has escaped regulation. The state agency that regulates financial institutions proposed limited regulations on the industry in the fall of 2000, but not limits on interest rates. Also, in Illinois, causes have a way of recycling, so the industry likely will be the target of further legislative attempts to curb its practices. However, ISLA seems to have taken a cue from the way ComEd and Illinois Power faced their deregulation dilemma. The industry has organized, contributed, and has thus become a force to be reckoned with when legislation affecting the industry comes before the legislature.

Was it only money that secured the Illinois Small Loan Association's spring 2000 legislative success?

Money is important; it does buy access. However, organization and full-time representation are also important, particularly when the opposition is not strong. Like the potential buyers of new cars, those who are or may be adversely affected by an unregulated small loan industry are unorganized, unrepresented, and without funds for campaign contributions. The legislature's tendency to serve the organized and to listen to the sound of money makes it difficult to champion the cause of the consumers over the industry. Contribution limits would lessen the advantage of the Illinois Small Loan Association, but it would not eliminate it.

Beyond once again illustrating the role of money in influencing the outcome of the legislative process, the payday loan case is troubling for two reasons. First is the short time frame in which ISLA raised and distributed its money, particularly to the legislative leaders. The direction of these relationships is often difficult to determine. Did the companies that fund the association decide that because they had an interest before the legislature that it was important to give to the leaders? Or is there an implicit or explicit expectation that those who have interests before the legislature must contribute to its leaders? There is a feeling among many longtime observers that the dynamic in Springfield has shifted from one in which making contributions helps to one where failing to make even nominal contributions hurts the chances of the individual or group with business before the legislature. The appearance or the suggestion of a "pay to play" system is just as corrosive to media and public support for the process as the reality of such a system. Contribution limits would provide a ceiling on what groups and individuals could give. But they also would provide a ceiling on how much the leaders or members could ask for. By limiting the amount that legislators could ask for, both the appearance and the possible reality of legislators pressuring interest groups for money could be mitigated.

The second troubling aspect of the ISLA case is that ISLA's contributions to the legislative leaders became known before the end of the spring session only because there was a primary election going on. Even though these contributions had nothing to do with elections, they had to be reported as part of the pre-election reports that were due before the March 2000 primary. If the legislative action and the coincidental contributions had been made during the 1999 spring legislative session, the industry's sudden urge to make political donations would not have been disclosed until July 31, 1999, long after the spring session had adjourned. The only way to make disclosure work for contributions that are directed at influencing policy during the time the legislature is in session is to require more frequent reporting that is oriented to the schedule of legislative activity as well as to the election schedule.

Gambling with Public Policy

The public's perception of the legislative process in Springfield is often that of a backroom game of "let's make a deal" politics dominated by powerful legislative leaders, the governor, and influential special interests who hire high-priced lobbyists and dole out huge campaign contributions. Though the scene smacks of smoke-filled rooms drawn by editorial cartoonists, there are times when that is a very accurate description of lawmaking in Illinois. The process that produced a 1999 law providing for the expansion of the gambling industry and subsidies for its major players was one of those times.

The case of the gambling expansion bill illustrates four points:

1. How campaign money flows to power.
2. How the current campaign finance reporting system makes it difficult to determine exactly who is giving how much.
3. How organized groups that coalesce can easily overrun an under-organized and under-funded opposition – even an opposition whose views are probably in sync with those of the majority of Illinois citizens.
4. How packing a bill with expensive goodies helps it become law.

No 1998 legislative or gubernatorial candidate ran on a platform calling for dramatically expanding casino gambling in the state. No one made subsidizing the horse racing industry the cornerstone of his or her television ads or direct mail pieces. There was no army of concerned citizens pressing for more horse racing, more casino gambling. More gambling was not at the top of any public opinion polls measuring the concerns of Illinois citizens as we moved into the twenty-first century. The gambling industry is sharply divided between casino and horse racing interests that are, in turn, fragmented into individual gambling facilities that compete with every other facility for the gambling dollar. Organized opponents of gambling expansion, while small in number and poorly funded, had intensity and unified organization on their side. In the theater of public opinion, they tended to come off as the "good guys in the white hats" versus the slick riverboat gamblers and the blue blood horse people. All of this hardly seems like a recipe for passing a gambling subsidy and expansion bill.

Except for the money. There was a huge amount of money to be made from expanding and subsidizing gambling. Just as important, there was a huge amount of money at the disposal of those who would benefit from the subsidies and expansion and a campaign finance system that allowed those with money to make maximum use of it. With the wide-open Illinois campaign finance system, those individuals, groups, and corporations seeking to use money to influence the passage of the gambling bill were able to contribute as much as they wanted to the political committees of elected public officials and candidates for public office. As a result, by the end of the 1999 spring legislative session, a bill was signed into law. The goodies included subsidies and tax breaks for horse racing tracks, dockside gambling for riverboat casinos, and the potential shifting of a casino license to the Village of Rosemont in Cook County.

Publicly sanctioned gambling has become a very big deal in Illinois. In 1999, wagers on legal gambling in Illinois exceeded $23.6 billion. Of that figure, more than $20 billion came from riverboat casinos. While the Illinois State Lottery is a public operation (run by the Illinois Department of the Lottery), horse racing and riverboat casinos are not. They are private operations that are licensed, regulated, and taxed by the state, making tracks and boats an important source of state and local revenue. Riverboat casinos, horse racing, and the state lottery generated more than $956 million in revenue for the state and local governments in 1999. With that kind of money at stake, gambling policy is obviously a legitimate matter of concern for the legislature, whether or not the industry contributes to political campaigns.

But the industry does have a history of making hefty contributions to the campaign funds of Illinois public officials. Private sector gambling interests divide into three primary groups: horse racing, existing riverboat casinos, and those seeking expansion of casino gambling. Between the beginning of 1993 and the end of 1999, horse racing interests contributed $2.38 million to legislative and statewide candidates; riverboat casino interests contributed $2.37 million; and those seeking riverboat casino expansion contributed $944,000. That is nearly $5.7 million in a seven-year period.

As with other politically savvy special interest groups, the three segments of the gambling industry have bet on the favorite by giving the majority of their contributions to the people with the most power. A comparison of contributions from gambling interests from 1993 to 1999 illustrates this point. In the 1993-1994 election cycle, when Governor Jim Edgar was winning re-election, he received $184,969 in contributions from gambling interests. For that same period, Secretary of State George Ryan was running for re-election. He got $57,250 in contributions from gambling interests. In the 1995-1996 cycle, the governor's office and the secretary of state's office were not up for re-election. That year, Edgar's take from the gambling industry dropped to $82,561, and Ryan took in $51,811. In 1997, Governor Edgar announced he would not run for re-election. His 1997-1998 contributions from gambling interests plummeted to $34,100. During that same period, Ryan became the presumptive favorite to win the Republican Party's nomination for governor and indeed was elected to the state's highest office. His contributions from gambling interests skyrocketed to $428,209, with a majority of those contributions received during the last six months of 1998. In 1999, Governor Ryan received an additional $58,500 from gambling interests. Governor Ryan's 1997-1998 total was more than eight times his total from the previous two years and more than twice what Governor Edgar received in the 1993-1994 election cycle from the same sources (see Figure 5.1). Part of the dramatic increase can be attributed to Governor Ryan's reputation as a dealmaker and to his somewhat ambiguous position during the campaign on the expansion of riverboat gambling. But the fact that a major piece of gambling-related legislation was in the offing also prompted the huge flow of gambling money into the campaign account of the soon-to-be governor.

The pattern with respect to the four legislative leaders is just as clear. Between 1993 and 1999, the four legislative leaders took more than $2.8 million in contributions from gambling interests. Of that total, the leaders received $914,000 in the 1997-1998 election cycle and an additional $323,000 in 1999, meaning that money poured in

FIGURE 5.1

**Money Flows to Power:
Campaign Contributions from Gambling Interests to the Governor/Governor-Elect, 1993-1998**

In hundred thousand dollar increments

GEORGE RYAN
$482,209

$184,969

$57,250

$82,561

JIM EDGAR
$34,100

$51,811

1993-1994   1995-1996   1997-1998

quickly as the favorable legislation was being considered in the state legislature. Senate President James "Pate" Philip and the Senate Republican campaign committee received a total of $267,000 from gambling interests in the 1997-1998 election cycle and an additional $89,000 in 1999. Senate Democratic Leader Emil Jones and the Senate Democratic campaign committee received $62,000 in the 1997-1998 election cycle and $37,000 in 1999. House Speaker Michael Madigan got a total of $123,000 from gambling interests in the 1997-1998 cycle and an additional $33,000 in 1999. House Republican Leader Lee Daniels and his House campaign committee took in $452,000 in the 1997-1998 election cycle and $164,000 in 1999. In addition, the State Republican Party received $111,000 in the 1997-1998 election cycle and $17,000 in 1999, while the State Democratic Party got $64,000 in the 1997-1998 cycle and $22,000 more in 1999.

Overall, only 25 percent ($1.43 million of $5.69 million) of gambling contributions from 1993 to 1999 went to rank-and-file legislators or legislative candidates. The other 75 percent went to the legislative leaders, the governor, the other constitutional officers, and the two state political parties. The primary lessons are that money flows to power and that interests with significant financial resources can bring them quickly to bear on the centers of power in Illinois politics.

Another lesson is instructive to political observers and campaign finance reformers. Tracking the contributions from gambling interests is a difficult proposition. First, the market is segmented into three parts: riverboat operators, those seeking riverboat licenses, and the state's horse racing industry.

Tracking contributions from Illinois' five riverboat operators is fairly straightforward. The Empress River Casino Corporation in Joliet is the largest contributor, with $303,000 given in the 1997-1998 cycle and $126,000 more in 1999. During the 1997-1998 election cycle Harrah's Casino Cruises in Joliet gave $106,000. Contributions from Hollywood Casino in Aurora, the Elgin Riverboat Resort, and the Casino Queen in East St. Louis came to more than $50,000 in the 1997-1998 election cycle.

It takes more homework and some judgment to uncover contribution amounts from people who are interested in riverboat gambling expansion. To do so requires an understanding of who the players are. For example, prior to 1999 only one individual and one group seeking casino gambling expansion were highly visible. Donald Stephens, a township committeeman and the Republican mayor of Rosemont, has actively supported Rosemont as a site for riverboat casino expansion. In the 1997-1998 election cycle, he and his township committee fund made more than $146,000 in campaign contributions to legislative and statewide officeholders and candidates. Riverboat casino expansion was not Mayor Stephens' only — or even primary — political concern, and many specific contributions were unrelated to promoting the expansion of casino gambling. (In all Stephens transferred more than $857,000 out of his campaign fund in the 1997-1998 period, with more than $700,000 going to local rather than state-level candidates and parties.) However, his general political influence within Cook County provided a strong base from which to pursue casino gambling expansion for Rosemont. In 1999, Stephens reported spending more than $525,000 out of his political committee fund with almost $95,000 going to legislative and statewide candidates. The other visible group seeking the expansion of casino gambling is the Lake County Riverboat Project, which is promoting Lake County as a site for a riverboat casino. The group contributed more than $59,000 in the 1997-1998 election cycle with the money primarily directed at the governor, the Republican legislative leaders, and the speaker of the House. In 1999, the Lake County group contributed more than $6,000 to legislative and statewide candidates.

A further complication arises when examining contributions from the horse racing industry. One large contributor is the National Jockey Club (associated with Sportsman's Park and owner Charles Bidwill). In the 1997-1998 election cycle, the National Jockey Club made $115,000 worth of political contributions. Other key players are the Illinois Harness Horse Racing Association and the Illinois Racing Association (associated with Balmoral Park). But by far, racing interests in Illinois are dominated by the companies and family members associated with the Duchossois name.

Over 70 percent of the horse racing contributions in the 1997-1998 election cycle came from Duchossois family members or companies owned or operated by Duchossois family members. With total 1997-1998 contributions of $683,132, the family is the biggest single contributor among all the state's gambling interests.

The magnitude and complexity of the campaign contributions from interests associated with the Duchossois family can be seen in Figure 5.2. At the time he made the contributions, Richard Duchossois was the owner of both Arlington International Racecourse and Hill N' Dale Farms. His son was president of Duchossois Industries, located at 845 Larch Avenue in Elmhurst, Illinois. Chamberlain Manufacturing and Thrall Car Manufacturing are both subsidiaries of Duchossois Industries. In addition, the DD-66 Corporation and three Duchossois family members who made campaign contributions all listed their address as 845 Larch Avenue in Elmhurst, Illinois, the address of Duchossois Industries. Assuming that these contributions share a common interest, the Duchossois companies and family members are the largest nonassociation or nongroup contributor to Illinois state-level political campaigns. In the 1997-1998 election cycle, only the Illinois State Medical Society, the Illinois Education Association, the Illinois Federation of Teachers, the Illinois Manufacturers' Association, and the Illinois Hospital and HealthSystems Association gave more.

With so much money pouring in from so many interests, one may wonder why a gambling expansion bill couldn't get through the legislature before 1999. That's where the concept of coalescence comes in.

Prior to 1999, the interests of the horse racing, riverboat casino, and casino expansion groups were generally in conflict. As a result, campaign contributions from gambling interests were not all pushing in the same direction in terms of trying to influence public policy. Horse racing interests wanted assistance from the state in the form of reduced taxes and direct subsidies to support what had become a stagnant industry. Pressure from riverboat casinos was hurting the horse racing industry in Illinois. The state's major racetrack, Arlington International Racecourse, suspended operations

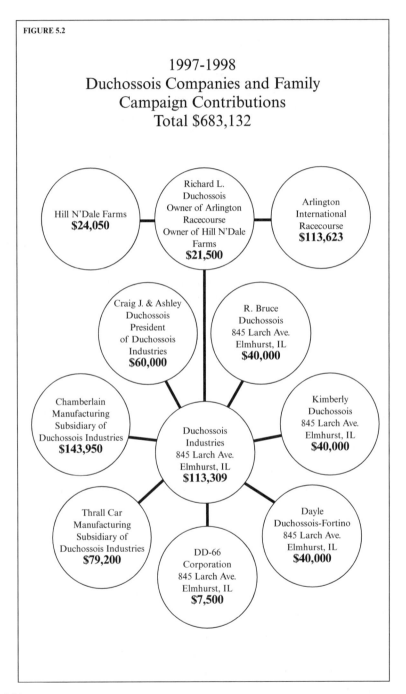

FIGURE 5.2

1997-1998
Duchossois Companies and Family
Campaign Contributions
Total $683,132

Hill N'Dale Farms
$24,050

Richard L. Duchossois
Owner of Arlington Racecourse
Owner of Hill N'Dale Farms
$21,500

Arlington International Racecourse
$113,623

Craig J. & Ashley Duchossois
President of Duchossois Industries
$60,000

R. Bruce Duchossois
845 Larch Ave.
Elmhurst, IL
$40,000

Chamberlain Manufacturing
Subsidiary of Duchossois Industries
$143,950

Duchossois Industries
845 Larch Ave.
Elmhurst, IL
$113,309

Kimberly Duchossois
845 Larch Ave.
Elmhurst, IL
$40,000

Thrall Car Manufacturing
Subsidiary of Duchossois Industries
$79,200

DD-66 Corporation
845 Larch Ave.
Elmhurst, IL
$7,500

Dayle Duchossois-Fortino
845 Larch Ave.
Elmhurst, IL
$40,000

for the 1998 and 1999 seasons due to concerns over its economic viability. In addition to seeking state assistance, horse racing interests
were opposed to the expansion of casino gambling, though there
was some sentiment for expansion if it included casino gambling
operations at horse racing tracks. The riverboat casino interests
were primarily concerned with resisting efforts to expand the number of casino gambling licenses and resisting efforts to raise state or
local taxes on their operations. The one positive legislative goal the
casinos all shared was that they wanted the legislature to allow them
to operate their gaming tables without actually having to sail their
boats. They were also opposed to any legislation that would
strengthen the horse racing industry. Those who wanted to increase
the number of riverboat casino licenses faced strong opposition
from the existing riverboat casinos and the horse racing interests.

At the beginning of 1999, gambling interests had tremendous
access to the governor and the legislative leaders based on a decade
of ever-increasing campaign contributions. But their influence was
severely limited by the seemingly conflicting goals of casinos, horse
racing, and those seeking an expansion of the number of casino
licenses. The conflict within the industry played into the hands of the
anti-gambling groups and faith-based organizations concerned with
the social costs of gambling. Though the anti-gambling groups were
voluntary associations with few financial resources, they had forced
gambling interests to address such problems as compulsive gambling.
The anti-gambling forces also played on the schism in the industry
itself. Those opposed to legalized gambling in general, and the
expansion of gambling in Illinois in particular, found allies among
horse racing and riverboat casino interests when proposals were
floated to bring a casino to Chicago or Cook County. The anti-gambling forces could count on the riverboat casinos to oppose legislation aimed at helping horse tracks. Conversely, they could count on
the horse tracks to oppose legislation aimed at helping the riverboat
casino industry. As long as the gambling industry as a whole continued to be fractionalized, prospects were good that the long-term
stalemate over changes in Illinois gambling policy would continue.

But all of this changed in the spring of 1999. The potential for a

145

grand coalition between the warring factions of the gambling interests always had been present in Illinois. Each of the groups had significant needs that could be addressed by changes in state law, and their past contributions gave them access. In 1999, the factions of the industry decided that they would deal with each other as well as the legislature.

A gambling deal depended on four critical factors:

1. Satisfying horse racing interests, particularly Duchossois: Track owners wanted increased state support or some tax relief in order to offset losses from declining on-track revenue and increasing operating costs. Some owners would have liked to bring casino gambling to racetracks.
2. Satisfying the owners of existing casino licenses. Income from their industry had flattened, and they did not want added competition from more casinos.
3. Finding a way to bring a casino license to Chicago or Cook County in a manner that would satisfy Chicago Mayor Richard Daley.
4. Crafting a bill that the legislature would pass and the governor would sign.

In politics, a tried and true strategy for passing a bill is to make sure that everyone gets a piece of the pie. With the potential economic benefit for gambling interests, the potential huge profits from a Cook County-based casino, and a booming state budget as a source of money to sweeten the deal, the pie was more than adequate to do the job.

The basics of the agreement were to provide tax breaks and subsidies to the horse racing industry, particularly the owners of horse racing tracks, and to allow dockside gambling for riverboats. Under the deal, the owners of the suspended casino license in East Dubuque would be allowed to move to the Village of Rosemont, which is in Cook County next to O'Hare Airport. But in order to make these things happen, promoters of the legislation had to add on a little booty. The side payments included:

- Taking revenue from the relocated boat and using it to fund criminal justice facilities in Cook County and renovations for the University of Illinois football stadium and other public athletic facilities.

- Requiring that the relocated casino license partially be minority or female owned.
- Providing $30 million over five years in general revenue funding for economic development in depressed communities.
- Adding on an agreement that the Village of Rosemont would share the local government portion of gambling tax revenue from the new casino with more than 70 cities and villages in Cook County.

In the eyes of everybody except gambling opponents and downstate legislators without a casino in their districts, the bill that the gambling industry helped put together in 1999 truly had a little something for everyone. Richard Duchossois got tax breaks for the Arlington track worth at least $9 million a year with the prospect of another $10 million in subsidies from the Rosemont casino. And the owners of Illinois' other horse racing tracks and the thoroughbred and harness racing industries also benefited. Existing casinos were able to keep their slots and tables going without taking the trouble to weigh the anchor. Mayor Stephens got a huge engine to drive economic development and activity in his community. The owners of the East Dubuque license were able to increase its value dramatically. Mayor Daley got a gambling facility in Cook County with all the attendant economic benefits plus a subsidy for county government operations. Minority legislators, who initially blocked the bill in the Senate, got money for economic development and diversity in the ownership of the transferred riverboat license. Legislative leaders and the governor finally were able to assist some of their most important campaign contributors.

In the end, this is a classic example of powerful interests and big money dominating the process with little regard for the overall public policy merits of the legislation. These were not a set of standalone, good ideas that happened to be in the same bill. In fact, most complex legislation contains a severability clause that provides that if some portion of the bill is found unconstitutional, the rest of the bill will continue in force. The gambling bill had an inseverability clause. If the courts invalidate the transfer of the casino license, then dockside gambling and tax breaks for horse track owners also will fall. The gambling interests did not trust each other or share their diverse goals, but the combination of access and influence and the huge potential financial payoff drove the deal and ultimately made it happen.

The danger when money and influence dominate policymaking is that important changes can be made without any serious public debate over the public policy issues involved. Is horse racing as operated in the 1990s a viable industry in this decade, even with massive public subsidies? Should Illinois facilitate a major expansion in the amount of casino gambling taking place? What are the implications of having (for all practical purposes) land-based casino gambling instead of riverboat excursion gambling? Having established casino gambling and having expanded it to Cook County, can further expansion be resisted? Should it be? What are the social costs of increasing gambling in Illinois and how do they compare to the economic benefits of gambling? These are important questions, but they were largely ignored in the process that produced the 1999 gambling bill.

Events since the gambling bill was signed into law suggest that the debate is far from over. Revenue from the newly docked riverboat casinos jumped dramatically as soon as the new law was implemented. Proponents of gambling expansion will take that as a clear indication that the market has not been saturated. A lawsuit was filed in state court by supporters of a casino for Lake County to block the transfer of the East Dubuque license to Rosemont. That litigation halted construction activity by the Rosemont group and led to an impasse before the Illinois State Gaming Board. If the courts throw out the 1999 gambling bill, the pressure to construct an even more extensive gambling expansion bill would be overwhelming.

In a related development, Richard Duchossois sold Arlington International Racecourse in the spring of 2000 to the corporation that owns Churchill Downs, home of the Kentucky Derby. The sale price was greater than $72 million. An additional $19 to $28 million will go to Duchossois if Arlington indeed does receive subsidies when the Rosemont casino becomes operative. Because Securities and Exchange Commission filings clearly indicated that discussion between Duchossois and the owners of Churchill Downs had taken place in 1998, legislators and the press raised questions about Duchossois' motives for closing Arlington and seeking state support. There is no question that the 1999 gambling bill significantly increased the value of the Arlington track.

The success of the 1999 gambling bill is a tribute to the power of money in Illinois politics. Money alone did not pass the bill, but the advantage in access and influence to those who have it over those who do not is painfully evident. Donations in the millions of dollars from the gambling industry did not guarantee that the 1999 gambling bill would become law. But it would not have become law without them.

When Contributions Lead to Scandal

Even under the current campaign finance system, when it comes to tracing and judging the influence of money in the Illinois process, at least this much can be said:

- Knowledgeable, persistent people can — after the fact — make a reasonable determination of who gave money to whom and draw their own conclusions about how those donations may have influenced legislation.
- Opposition groups at least have the opportunity to try to organize and raise money to compete with the established special interest groups.
- The legal system can — and has — struck down legislation passed in violation of the state's constitution.
- "Dumb laws" can be revisited and changed by the legislature.

It's quite another matter, however, when a *quid pro quo* is at work and the execution of public policy becomes corrupted for personal and political gain. As noted earlier, the history of Illinois politics is a history of political scandal. In the 1990s, Illinois government faced two more scandals, the MSI case and the selling of commercial driver's licenses. Allegations that bribes were made under the guise of campaign contributions were central to both cases.

149

When Contributors Get Sweet Deals: The MSI Case

In the early 1990s, Management Services of Illinois, Inc. (MSI) had been good to its friends in high places. In an admitted attempt to gain influence and get state contracts (Pearson and Parsons 1997), between 1990 and 1995 the company and its key executives donated more than $310,000 in cash and computer services to Governor Jim Edgar's campaign fund. At the same time, campaign funds controlled by Senate President James "Pate" Philip took in more than $94,000 from MSI. Funds controlled by House Minority Leader Lee Daniels got $36,100 from MSI sources, and then-Secretary of State George Ryan received $26,000. In all, MSI-related contributions to executive officers and legislative officials topped half a million dollars for the five-year period.

The firm's strategy proved to be a good one. In 1991, the Illinois Department of Public Aid hired MSI on a no-bid contract to help find people who were double dipping by receiving Medicaid health care coverage while they also were covered under a private health insurance plan. Under the terms of the original agreement, MSI kept 19 percent of the amount the state recovered from the private insurance companies. In 1993, the final year of the contract, MSI earned $409,000 from the deal.

When the contract came up for renegotiation, the company gave some Department of Public Aid employees who were administering the contract lavish gifts, including trips to Puerto Rico and Palm Springs and gambling money to be used on a Joliet riverboat (Long 2000, Pearson and Parsons 1997). The immediate outcome was a contract in which MSI received $350 for each person it identified as having private insurance. Company income from the state contract ballooned to $11.2 million in 1994 (Long 1998). But the benefits to the department were greatly exceeded by the costs of the new contract, which had been approved by a number of agency officials and by the governor's office.

In the long run, however, the gifts and overpayments caught up to the company and the department. In May 1995, Michael Lawrence, who was at that time Governor Edgar's press secretary, got an anonymous letter alerting him to possible corruption in the MSI contract.

That led to an investigation of the circumstances surrounding the contract renegotiation. In August 1997, MSI, MSI co-founder Michael Martin, and Ronald Lowder, a state worker who oversaw the MSI contract, were found guilty on charges of bribing two mid-level public aid officials. No high-level officials were charged in the investigation, but prosecutors considered Governor Edgar's deputy chief of staff and his patronage director unindicted co-conspirators (Long 2000). And when Edgar took the stand in March 1997, it was the first time in 75 years that a sitting governor had testified as a subpoenaed defense witness in a criminal trial (Pearson and Parsons 1997).

The trial that convicted Michael Martin failed to convict MSI's other co-founder, William Ladd. In a *Chicago Tribune* story, Ladd's attorney, J. Steven Beckett, said that Ladd didn't know much about the gift giving, but offered: "The way he [Governor Edgar] handles the contractors, the way he handles business, the way his departments handle business, can only lead somebody like Bill Ladd into the feeling that this is all right, this is the way business is done in state government" (Pearson and Parsons 1997). Apparently defense attorneys were not the only ones who held this opinion. A juror who acquitted Ladd in August 1997 explained things this way: "It comes down to 'You scratch my back, I'll scratch yours.' They may not do anything against the law, but it's still wrong" (Pearson and Parsons 1997).

Following Martin's conviction and those of two low-level bureaucrats at the department, the U.S. attorney's office tried an upper-management official, James Berger, for public corruption in the administration of the MSI contract. Berger had been responsible for approving changes in the contract and for overseeing its implementation. Berger was the man responsible to the head of the agency and, ultimately, to the governor's office. He was also linked to the Senate president's office, which also has considerable influence over state agencies because of the way legislative leaders dominate the budget appropriations process.

The U.S. attorney's office never contended that Berger received any personal gain or accepted campaign contributions from MSI, but did see him as being motivated by a desire to please his political superiors and further his career in state government. As such, the U.S. attorney's office saw him as the link between corruption at the bottom and what prosecutors felt was illegal influence peddling at the top. Prosecutors looked at the bribes to bureaucrats, contributions to Governor Edgar's campaign fund and to Senate President Philip's campaign funds, and a contract revision that was extremely favorable to MSI while being extremely unfavorable to the agency, and they inferred a connection. The terms of the contract were so suspect that the U.S. attorney's office assumed that, short of gross incompetence, corruption was the only plausible explanation for the approval of the changes in the contract. Given the choice of being knaves or fools, officials within the agency and the governor's office chose the latter. A public admission of incompetence is not a great resumé builder, but it's not an indictable offense.

Berger was acquitted on all counts. Money and gifts changing hands in exchange for favorable treatment is an easy concept to explain to a jury, even if it is actually difficult to prove. Influence buying, the *quid pro quo* through campaign contributions, is more difficult to articulate to a jury and much more difficult to prove. A state bureaucrat's personal bank account has only one purpose; an Illinois campaign fund has many. Whatever the merit (if any) of the U.S. attorney's office's theory of the MSI case, it was unable to convict Berger, and no one else was indicted.

For campaign finance reformers, the importance of the MSI case isn't the fact that the investigation wound up convicting two Department of Public Aid employees and both MSI co-founders (Ladd was later convicted of money laundering charges) or that Edgar subsequently signed a purchasing reform bill requiring the three top officials in each agency to sign off on contracts worth more than $250,000. MSI is important because the MSI owners saw campaign contributions as a normal and proper way to facilitate landing a state contract. It wasn't such a great leap to think that a gift here or a trip there would allow them to increase their profits. In fact, according to Ladd, the company-hired lobbyists Terry Logsdon and Terry Bedgood advised the company that gifts and contributions were how business was transacted in Springfield. Logsdon and

Bedgood, who were later named as unindicted co-conspirators, were in a position to know Springfield's political culture. They were insiders who had worked for Governor Jim Thompson. Ladd testified that Bedgood arranged a meeting with Governor Edgar at which four MSI officials pledged $10,000 each and that Bedgood vetoed MSI's planned $35 fruit basket Christmas gifts in favor of gifts of steaks and lobsters. Berger was on that Christmas list (Finke 2000).

While the U.S. attorney's office was not able to draw the legal connection between huge campaign contributions at the top and gifts and bribes at the bottom, the general public has no trouble assuming — even expecting — that the connection is there. Regular patronage (jobs for political supporters) and pinstripe patronage (state contracts for corporate sponsors) has been an integral part of Illinois state politics for a long time (Freedman 1994). So has a wide-open campaign finance system. When the two get intertwined, it brings out the very worst of our political system. The personal costs to those who get caught are great, but the damage done to the legitimacy of the political process in the eyes of every citizen is even greater.

Bribes for Licenses

In the late fall of 1994 on Highway 94 just outside Milwaukee, Wisconsin, truck driver Ricardo Guzman lost a taillight assembly from his rig. Reverend Duane Willis was on that road that same day. He was driving a van that hit Guzman's debris. The taillight assembly tore into the van's gas tank and exploded Willis's van. Reverend Willis and his wife, Janet, survived the crash. Their six children did not (Gibson 1999).

In September 1999, Gonzolo Mendoza pleaded guilty to charges stemming from Operation Safe Road, a federal investigation that had established a pattern of corruption in Chicago-area truck driver's license examination facilities. Mendoza said that in 1992 he paid bribes so that several drivers could obtain their licenses fraudulently. One of those drivers, he said, was Ricardo Guzman (O'Connor 1999). As the federal investigation continued, two other drivers who got their licenses under suspicious circumstances in

153

Illinois were found to have been involved in fatal accidents in Maryland and California (*Illinois Issues*, April 2000).

Operation Safe Road began in 1998. The scope of the investigation spread quickly. Within two years, five testing facilities were found to have participated in the bribes-for-licenses scheme. By February 2000, more than 1,000 truck drivers had been asked to retake their driver's tests. And, as of August of that year, 37 people had been charged, and 28 of them had been found guilty (*Illinois Issues*, September 2000).

The probe was particularly troubling for Governor George Ryan. As the secretary of state during the time that most of the bribes took place, he was the chief executive in charge of the agency that fraudulently issued the licenses. One of the defendants was Dean Bauer, whom Ryan hired as inspector general for the secretary of state when Ryan held that office. Bauer reported directly to Secretary Ryan. Federal investigators charged that, as inspector general, Bauer failed to investigate corruption in the department. A more troubling aspect is where the bribe money went. Some certainly landed in the pockets of the corrupt truck driving school instructors and secretary of state employees. But $170,000 was used to purchase fundraising tickets for George Ryan (*Illinois Issues*, March 2000). Mary Ann Mastrodomenico, the manager of the Melrose Park testing facility, pleaded guilty to racketeering charges in November 1998. She alone sold $50,000 in campaign fundraising tickets (United States Attorney).

Pressure on state employees to sell campaign fundraising tickets did not cause the driver's license selling scandal at the secretary of state's office. Public corruption in the conduct of governmental administrative duties is as old as the Republic. Most of the bribe money went into the pockets of those selling the licenses. For many of those indicted, buying political fundraising tickets never entered their mind. But in Illinois, pressuring public employees to sell and buy fundraising tickets is a time-honored tradition (Freedman 1994). (The provision in the 1998 campaign finance reform act prohibiting soliciting or receiving campaign contributions on state property was partially motivated by the practice of state agency personnel circumventing the law against doing political work on state time by declaring that they were on break and then selling tickets from their desks in the middle of the work day.)

What took place in the truck driver's testing facilities wasn't cause and effect. It was a coming together of two separate streams of corruption for those involved in the driver's license selling scandal. The bribe money allowed them to kill two birds with one stone: make money and curry political favor with their supervisors. Some felt pressure. Others embraced an opportunity.

Governor Ryan, who was not charged in the first two-and-a-half years of the investigation, denied suggestions that secretary of state employees' careers depended on their ability to sell the tickets (Grumman and Garza 1999). But he did admit that bribery was common at some facilities during his eight-year term as secretary of state. "It was there when I was there, probably going to be there in the future. It's a part of the culture there, I guess" (Long and Parsons 2000).

As this book went to press, the investigation was ongoing. But the probe had lasted long enough to uncover a culture of corruption at the department.

Would tighter campaign contribution and stricter reporting requirements have prevented the bribes-for-licenses scheme?

Possibly, but not necessarily. Corruption can occur in the best of environments.

Would stricter laws have diminished the culture of corruption?

Quite probably. In any event, the connection between the bribes and campaign contributions did not engender public confidence in the current campaign finance system. In fact, the scheme may easily prove to be a very hard swipe at politics as usual in this state. It's one thing for politicians to pick up campaign contributions from people seeking special legislation. But it's a grave matter indeed when public employees put dangerous drivers on the road because they feel the need to contribute heavily to their political bosses.

Money and Policy in Illinois

Corruption will not disappear if Illinois enacts better campaign finance and reporting laws. And, even with better campaign finance

155

regulation, "dumb laws," as my daughter calls them, still may get passed.

Under the current system, money is not the only reason that one side wins and the other side loses. Every bill that the legislature passes and the governor signs has a public policy content. (The boilerplate language in the 1999 gambling bill stressed the need for economic development and the importance of horse racing as agribusiness.)

But money is critically important, both in terms of campaign contributions and the hiring of lobbyists to push legislation. One of the supporters of the 1999 gambling bill talked about having 100 lobbyists working on it. Even if you halve that figure, the impact of such an effort is critical. The cost of hiring 50 lobbyists is beyond the means of most interest groups.

It's easy to lose sight of the public policy content of some issues when special interest groups with big money and organization square off against other rich and well-organized special interest groups. When unrepresented or underrepresented interests oppose well-organized, well-funded interests, the potential for distortion and bias in public policy jumps drastically. The result is often one-sided, with outcomes ranging from the dramatic — the 1999 gambling bill and the 1999 Wirtz liquor distributor bill — to the quiet — the legislature's inaction in 1999 on payday loan industry regulation. As one longtime incumbent legislator put it, "I like to remain the people's representative. The trouble is that the people don't have any money."

There is nothing wrong with organizing and donating. They are important, integral, and constitutionally protected parts of the American democratic process. But, under the current campaign finance system and political climate in Illinois, making the kind of contributions that often are necessary to have a voice in public policy debates is beyond the means of many. As this chapter and the one preceding it clearly show, the role of money in Illinois politics is increasingly negative. It is time for a change. The next chapter offers 14 ideas designed to open the Illinois election and policymaking processes to more voices, even if those voices emanate from people with fewer dollars in their pockets.

Changing the Political Culture

Is Illinois Ready
for Reform?

Illinois politics is not for the faint of heart. Nor, as the preceding chapters show, is it for the thin of wallet. Money is often critically important in elections and policymaking in Illinois. At best, money in politics is merely corrosive to public support for the political process. At worst, it is corrupting to the people involved in the state's political processes as well as the outcomes of those processes. Naturally, identifying the problems that the totally unrestricted flow of money causes in the political process in Illinois is much easier than formulating solutions. Except for true believers on both sides of the debate, it is not clear exactly where we should be going or how we should get there.

The Evolving Status Quo

Doing nothing is a strategy. The lesson of the last quarter of the 20th century is that, left alone, the state's political culture will adapt to the times with the essence of Illinois politics remaining unchanged. Since 1975, we have graduated from a party-centered political and electoral process run by party bosses and a small set of interest groups to a candidate-centered political process ruled by the legislative leaders, the governor, and largely the same small set of interest groups. A critical factor in this transition has been the growing importance of money to those who run for office or control the conduct of elections aided by the growing power of those private interests who supply that money. What has not changed are the primary goals of the Illinois politicians: winning elections and getting power. Often this means officeholders end up granting patronage favors, engineering policy advantages, and protecting opportunities for financial rewards for those who support Illinois politicians.

The resilience of Illinois' political culture and power structure is amazing. The last major changes in the political process achieved by an Illinois governor were the adoption of annual state budgets, an executive budget process, and a state income tax under Governor Richard Ogilvie from 1970 to 1972. The citizens of Illinois rewarded him by turning him out of office in the election of 1972, making him a Republican governor who couldn't ride Richard Nixon's broad coattails (Pensoneau 1997). The post-Watergate campaign finance reform movement that swept the country hardly made a ripple in Illinois, marked only by the passage of a limited disclosure law in 1976.

However, twice in recent history significant changes in the processes of the Illinois General Assembly occurred. The first came after all 177 members were elected in a court-ordered at-large election in 1964, after the legislature failed to redistrict (Everson 1996). A 1980 amendment to the Illinois Constitution eliminated cumulative voting for the Illinois House and the reduced the size of that body from 177 to 118 members starting with the 1982 elections. Legislative districts were also redrawn with the result that all legislative candidates had to run in new districts, but "politics as usual" hardly skipped a beat (Wheeler 1982). The new legislature in 1983 did not advance any major changes in the process or produce any significant policy reforms. Instead, single-member districts and the evolving technology of political campaigning combined to provide the legislative leaders with an opportunity to centralize their power. Soon, leaders took control of all the competitive elections in the districts. Of course, they have always had control over the legislative process in Springfield. Virtually unlimited access to private money and unlimited freedom in using money in campaigns has been a constant and critical factor in this development (Redfield 1998).

The policy implications of the way money reinforces Illinois' leader-dominated, status quo-oriented politics were detailed in Chapter 5. For 30 years, social and political reformers from the right and the left have felt frustrated with the pragmatism and lack of ideological commitment of those holding political power, regardless of who those people were. Those politicians have responded to calls for such bricks-and-mortar programs as Governor Jim Thompson's Build Illinois in 1986 and Governor George Ryan's Illinois First in 1999. But calls for social reform — be it the Equal Rights Amendment, gay rights, restrictions on abortion rights, school finance reform, or school vouchers — have gone largely unheard. Add campaign finance reform to the list. Because it is about fundamental changes in the state's political process, there is no way to make things right with another road project.

From this perspective, the basic inertia and pragmatism of Illinois politics make campaign finance reform problematic. First, those in control and those who compete for control have a vested interest in maintaining a status quo that allows them maximum freedom to get and spend money. Second, there is virtually no backlash against legislators who remain silent on the topic of campaign finance reform. There are not many single-issue voters driven by the cause, and the cynicism of the press and the public ensures that all politicians and their parties share equally in the blame for the excesses and outrages of the current, wide-open system. So, at the most basic level, for politicians there is no clear disadvantage from tacitly keeping things as they are and no advantage to be won by being identified with reform efforts. The advantages and potential advantages of operating within the system are real and obvious to the elected officials and interest groups that control the current system, as well as to those with the financial resources to compete for control. And political advantage, not sterling public policy, is all too often the driving force behind Illinois government.

Getting It Together: The Context of Reform

Yet even in this risk-averse political environment, campaign finance reform advocates have managed to make small but mighty inroads. In fact, it is tempting for those favoring reform to look at increased disclosure, new ethics laws, increased media attention, and particularly electronic filing and public access to campaign records via the Internet as the beginning of a major change in the way that money operates in Illinois politics. As a result of reform measures in 1997 and 1998, there has been a huge increase in the amount of information available and a dramatic reduction in the time and effort required to access that information. If the news media, public interest groups, candidates, and concerned citizens use the technology, the results should be increased understanding and scrutiny of money's role in Illinois politics. Expecting this outcome doesn't require a very large leap of faith. Unfortunately, translating height-

ened awareness into the actions necessary to bring about fundamental changes in the current "cash and carry" system of Illinois
politics will require more than faith and good intentions.

At a minimum, those advocating campaign finance reform must
agree on a common set of goals and a unified strategy. Prior to 1998,
reform groups in Illinois spent as much time fighting each other over
strategy and policy differences as they did fighting for change.
Efforts to find common ground produced a more united front in the
1999-2000 legislative session. Still, achieving concensus in the current debate over campaign finance reform is no easy task. At one
extreme are those reformers who live in a world where politics is an
evil that corrupts the governmental processes and distorts the outcome of elections. For them, private money is a tool of politics. As
such, they see a fundamental contradiction between private money
and public elections, between private money and public policy. In an
ideal world, we would elect the best people for the job, people who
would then make decisions based on merit, not on politics, particularly not on politics fueled by private money. To an idealist, the current campaign finance system, in Illinois and nationally, is a disas-
ter. The result is a process awash with private money, with elections
and policy going to the highest bidder. From the perspective of idealist reformers, nothing short of full public financing of elections
and the extreme curtailment or (better still) total elimination of private money in the political process will clean up government.
Idealists see those who would stand pat as professional politicians
or political hacks who want to keep the ways and means of political
power bottled up all for themselves.

At the other extreme of the debate are those politicians and insiders who see winning as the only goal of politics. Politics is war, and
war justifies any means necessary. Policy and money are means to an
end, tools to be used efficiently and effectively. From this perspective, the perfect system is the free flow of money in a free market
with the grudging acceptance of as little disclosure as possible. In
this light, the current campaign finance system in Illinois is close to
perfect and vastly better than the reformers' ideal. Defenders of this
system cite the First Amendment, free speech, and the right to peti-

tion government. But far from these altruistic concerns, their agenda is more likely a commitment to the status quo because it works for those who have power and those who can compete for power in the current system. Many of the strongest opponents of campaign finance reform see reformers as impotent amateurs who probably don't understand most of the political process and who are too easily (and perhaps wrongly) offended by what they do understand.

In the middle are politicians, public and private interest groups, and citizens who are fundamentally troubled by the role that money plays in the political process, but at odds over what the real problems are and how to address them. They wonder: What are the problems? Are all elections too costly, or just some, or none? Is declining voter participation a problem? Is a lack of opponents, or a lack of competition, or the difficulty of defeating incumbents problems? If so, what role does money play? Do political leaders have too much money and too much freedom to use it in elections and, as a result, too much power? Does money sometimes drive the public agenda? Does it distort the policy process? All of these questions have been raised as criticisms of the role of money in the Illinois system.

If there is a problem, what is to be done? Is more complete disclosure the answer? More timely disclosure? Contribution limits? Limits on how much money legislative leaders or parties can spend on individual campaigns? Prohibitions on contributions from regulated industries? Prohibitions on direct corporate or union contributions? Voters guides? Free mailings for every candidate? Full or partial public financing of legislative campaigns or campaigns for governor? Voluntary spending limits tied to public financing? All of these solutions have been offered up as cures for the ills of Illinois politics.

To move campaign finance reform forward requires some agreement on what changes would be necessary to address specific practices or conditions and a clear understanding of the impact that addressing one element of the system would have on other parts of the system. Campaign finance reform is a complex puzzle without a single solution. While it is true that those with political power largely believe the status quo should be preserved, a lack of political clout or political will is not the only reason change has been so difficult to achieve in Illinois. Those seeking reform are often at odds over goals and strategy.

Competing Goals and
the Campaign Finance Reform Movement

Making changes in the role money plays in the political process is ultimately about the relationship between citizens and the political process. The health of our political system depends on two related factors: increasing participation in the political process and restoring public confidence.

How to get there is what the campaign finance reform debate is all about. The goals usually advanced for campaign finance reform are:

- Increasing competition in elections.
- Reducing financial barriers to participation by candidates.
- Reducing the influence of private campaign contributions from groups and individuals on the outcome of elections.
- Reducing the influence of private campaign contributions from groups and individuals on shaping and implementing public policy.
- Reducing the dominance of legislative leaders over legislative elections and legislative policymaking.
- Increasing voter information.
- Increasing the public accountability of candidates and contributors.

In the abstract, these are all worthy goals and achieving them would help restore confidence in the political process and increase citizen participation. However, when we turn these goals into specific changes in the political process, we often find they are incompatible. Cost versus competition is a good example. When we get to specifics, we may find that making some Illinois elections more competitive may make all Illinois elections more expensive. Conversely, making all Illinois elections less expensive may make some Illinois elections less competitive.

Almost half of all the winners in legislative elections faced no opponents in the 1998 general election. If we consider this a problem, then we could decide that the solution would be to pass a law that provides a modest system of public financing grants to all candidates who win their party primaries. Grants at the $50,000 level would probably increase the number of candidates above the number that would have run in the general election without the grant. And, the grants might raise the visibility of those who would have run without the them. Additionally, such a grant might raise the viability of those who would have run without it. But, beware the unintended consequences. The idea would create a cost to the state somewhere in the neighborhood of $17.7 million per election, assuming full participation in an election following redistricting. And, the $50,000 may not even be enough to make visible campaigns, let alone viable campaigns in which the challenger actually has a chance to win. Finally, this system would make the campaign funds of all candidates, including safe and even unopposed incumbents, $50,000 richer. So the outcome might well be a system producing more candidates and higher campaign costs with no guarantee of more actual competition.

Does this mean public financing is a bad idea for Illinois? Not necessarily. I used this hypothetical case to illustrate that the role of money in politics is a complex, multifaceted question and to suggest that no solution can be perfect. Reform-minded groups and individuals need to consider the goals of campaign finance reform. And, they must realize that in order to achieve even one — no matter how seemingly minor — it will be necessary to allow for trade-offs between competing goals and their unintended consequences.

It is this fear of unintended consequences that makes even sympathetic incumbent politicians cling to the status quo. Politics in general and Illinois politics in particular is anti-risk. Any *major* changes in the way money operates within the Illinois political system are bound to have effects that neither proponents nor opponents expect. Even those politicians and pundits who are the most uncomfortable with the current system in Illinois may be reluctant to trade a certain, though unpleasant, reality for an uncertain future. This is not a dynamic for fundamental changes in the way we do politics in Illinois.

Redfield's Reform Recommendations

After spending the entire book detailing the problems and excesses of the current system, which allows for cozy alliances between campaign contributors and policymakers, it's now time to turn to some recommendations for change. I know the following policy proposals will strike some as unnecessarily timid or incomplete. But underlying them is a firm belief that contributions from private citizens to political campaigns are a legitimate form of political participation that should be encouraged. Like all forms of participation, private contributions can be abused. They need to be monitored and regulated. But it is neither desirable nor politically feasible to eliminate them. Also underlying these policy recommendations is the assumption that a frontal assault on the current campaign system in Illinois is doomed to failure in the short run. Even if reformers were sure of the ultimate solution, political leaders and private interests who dominate Illinois politics can defeat major reform. The constitutional framework in Illinois does not allow any kind of citizen initiative process to bypass the legislature and put comprehensive campaign finance reform directly to a popular vote. The only changes that will take place in Illinois' campaign finance law are those supported by the legislative leaders, approved by the General Assembly, and signed into law by the governor. So, all of us in the reform community must understand this reality: Change is most likely to come from working on the margins of the political process and the political culture. It will be slow going, and it is likely to produce only incremental changes in the short term.

The only hope for dramatic change in the immediate future is an unexpected political or social event that provides an opportunity to redefine the basic nature of Illinois politics. The licenses-for-bribes scandal in the secretary of state's office that was coming to light in the year 2000 could prove to be such an event. Or, controversy over the amount of money in elections for Supreme Court and appellate judges may provide an opportunity. But outside of changing the nature of judicial elections, I think the short-term prospect for radical change is not good. However, the 1997 and 1998 campaign finance inroads have taught two lessons: It is possible to build momentum for ethics and campaign finance issues; and change becomes cumulative.

In the next few pages I offer 14 recommendations for campaign finance reform in Illinois. None of these ideas, by itself, is earth-shattering. But, taken as a whole, these changes would help restore public confidence in the political process and increase participation. They would increase competition and reduce financial barriers for candidates. They would reduce the influence of money on the outcome of elections and on the shaping and implementation of public policy. Finally, they would increase voter information and the public accountability of candidates and contributors.

Recommendations on Contribution Limits

The essence of the Illinois system in the year 2001 is that anyone can give directly to a candidate or elected official and anyone can give as much as he or she wants. But, placing reasonable limits on how much someone can contribute would go a long way in reducing both the actual corruption and the appearance of corruption that pervade Illinois politics. Reasonable limits on contributions would restore some balance to the system and remove a major source of the cynicism of the general public and the news media toward Illinois' political system.

Redfield Reform Recommendation

 # 1 *Contributions from individuals, candidate committees, party committees, and non-candidate committees should be limited to $5,000 during a two-year period; no more than $2,500 prior to a primary election, and no more than $2,500 prior to a general election from a single source and for the office held or sought.*

Corruption and the appearance of corruption go with large contributions. Under current Illinois law, Bill Gates or the Microsoft
Corporation could give one of the legislative leaders a billion dollars
to finance the next round of elections. The leaders then would, as
they typically do, provide hundreds of thousands of dollars to legislative candidates in targeted races.

Though the Bill Gates scenario is partly facetious, traditionally in
Illinois a few interest groups, individuals, and corporations make
contributions in the $10,000 to $100,000 range to individual legislative leaders and in the hundreds of thousands of dollars to individual candidates for statewide office. In contrast, most contributions
to a candidate or party committee typically come from contributions of less than $5,000 during a two-year election cycle. So, the
impact of modest limits in the $5,000 range on the contribution
behavior for most individuals, interest groups, and corporations
would have little to no effect on most candidates. But, for legislative
leaders, constitutional officers, and a few individuals, corporations,
and associations, the impact of $5,000 contribution limits would be
dramatic, severely curtailing their influence on elections and the
public policy process.

In addition to the argument for reducing corruption or the
appearance of corruption of elected officials, contribution limits
also restrict the amount of money that elected officials can com-
mand from groups, individuals, and corporations with interests
before government. For example, the small loan association (representing payday loan companies) raised $85,000 in late 1999 and
early 2000 and gave more than $10,000 to each of the legislative
leaders in February and March of 2000 during a time when bills to
regulate the industry were before the legislature. Did the small loan
association decide that they had interests before the legislature and
choose to contribute money to advance those interests? Did the legislative leaders send indirect signals that people with an interest
before the legislature are expected to contribute to the leaders?
Whatever the relationship, a modest contribution limit of $2,500
before the primary would have significantly reduced the amount
that payday and title loan companies contributed to the leaders.

Contribution limits can serve as a restraint on both interest groups seeking influence and elected officials seeking contributions.

Redfield Reform Recommendation

2 *Candidates for office should be limited to having only one campaign committee, and party organizations should have just one committee at the local, county, legislative, and statewide levels. Finally, corporations, unions, and associations should be allowed to form only one political action committee.*

In order to make contribution limits work, both those contributing and those receiving contributions must be prohibited from forming multiple political committees to give or receive contributions. Political parties are key elements in the organization of Illinois politics. They are intermediate institutions that provide people both the opportunity to participate in politics and to have a larger voice in elections and policy-making. The geographic bases of party organizations in Illinois is a fact of life. So, party organizations should be allowed to form separate committees at the local, county, and state levels, but they should be limited to one committee at each level. Political parties within the legislature serve the same functions. Each party caucus in each chamber of the legislature should be permitted to form only one legislative chamber committee.

Redfield Reform Recommendation

3 *Ban direct contributions from corporations and unions.*

The core of the political process is participation of the individual. Corporations and unions cannot vote, and they should not contribute. This has been the standard in federal elections for corporations and banks since 1907 and unions since 1943. It is a good one. This ban would not prohibit corporations or unions from organizing political action committees to which members, employees, officers, and stockholders could make voluntary contributions. And those political action committees would be allowed to contribute to candidates and party committees.

A Recommendation on Spending Limits

Earlier in the chapter, I talked about making choices about campaign finance reform goals. I have also discussed the law of unintended consequences and outlined the state's political culture. These considerations weigh into my sole recommendation concerning campaign spending limits.

Redfield Reform Recommendation

#4 *Reformers should abandon efforts to directly limit candidate spending on political campaigns unless there is a significant change in the rulings of the U.S. Supreme Court.*

Given Supreme Court decisions regarding independent expenditures and so-called issue ads, spending limits are an illusion, even with complete public financing.

Recommendations on Judicial Elections

The issues of who funds judicial campaigns and what role those contributions play in both the public's perception of the administration of justice and the actual administration of justice call into question the whole idea of electing judges under the same rules that apply to local and state legislative and administrative offices. The case at the appellate and Supreme Court levels is clear. There is no reason to expect that these problems do not extend to the circuit court level.

Redfield Reform Recommendation

#*5* *Appoint rather than elect judges.*

We should not be electing judges at the trial court, appellate court, or Supreme Court level. The appearance of corruption, of the ability to buy access to the bench, is damaging to the integrity of the judicial system. Public support of that system is critical to administering justice. The huge amounts of money being spent to run for some judicial offices and the potential conflict of interest associated with judicial candidates' acceptance of contributions from law firms and corporations were documented in Chapter 4. Failure to act on this recommendation will only worsen the picture of a justice system that appears to be for sale.

Redfield Reform Recommendation

#*6* *As an alternative to appointing judges, provide full public funding and place $250 contribution limits per election for these races.*

If we are going to keep electing judges, then we need to take steps to reduce the corruption and the appearance of corruption that come with a wide-open campaign finance system. Severely limiting how much people and organizations can give and providing sufficient public money to run judicial campaigns would eliminate the need for candidates to raise huge sums of money. These changes would also alleviate the temptation for law firms and corporations to use big contributions to leverage access to, and favor from, Illinois judges.

Recommendations on Public Financing

For many in the reform movement, full public funding of campaigns linked to spending limits is the only meaningful reform worth pursuing. Under the banner of "clean money," the public financing movement has scored a small number of recent successes in getting states to adopt comprehensive systems of public financing for legislative and statewide elections. All but one came through the citizen initiative process. If these systems are successfully implemented, they will add momentum to the public financing movement in Illinois.

As a practical matter, the public financing of elections currently faces two hurdles in Illinois. The first is public acceptance. Much of the success in getting Illinoisans interested in public funding initiatives has come under the more socially acceptable name of "clean money" initiatives for financing campaigns. Even under this guise, there is still significant public resistance to public financing of elections. The second and more significant problem in Illinois is the absence of a citizen initiative process that can be used to enact changes in the law by bypassing the state legislature. In the short run, it will not be possible to convince a majority of state legislators, the legislative leaders, or an incumbent governor that legislative or statewide elections in Illinois should be publicly funded. But, with or without spending limits, it may be possible to provide a modest amount of public funding for all legislative candidates and candidates for statewide offices, if we define public funding as providing public resources to candidates.

Redfield Reform Recommendation

#7 *Provide public funding for two mailings to every household in an election district for any legislative or statewide office candidate who agrees to participate in two public debates and to abide by the promises of the Code of Fair Campaign Practices.*

This proposal would increase public discourse and public interest in elections. The secondary impact would be to put more resources in the hands of all candidates, thereby increasing competition. While this is a modest step, it would increase the number of candidates and the level of competition. The selling points of this idea for incumbents are: (1) the very fact that this idea *is* a modest one, and (2) the idea provides support for incumbents as well as challengers.

Redfield Reform Recommendation

#8 *The state should publish, in conjunction with county and municipal authorities, a voters guide prior to every public election.*

This voters guide would be sent to every household in the election district and would contain candidate pictures and information, candidate statements, and information about voting registration and participation. Voters guides would also explain any tax levies or other initiatives appearing on the upcoming ballot. The goal is to

173

increase information about the election. By spending money on these voters guides, the state would signal to its citizens — in a very tangible way — that official state policy is to encourage voting. Voters guides also would be useful to all legislative candidates and to candidates in statewide elections because they would put their names and their messages before the public at public expense.

Recommendations for Increased Reporting

The cornerstone of any system of regulating money in the political process is disclosure and reporting. Citizens, political activists, and the news media cannot make judgments about relationships involving campaign contributions if those relationships are not part of the public record. In terms of both elections and public policy decisions, it is more valuable to have such information before rather than after the fact. While Illinois has come a long way in a very short time, the existing system needs to be strengthened in terms of accountability.

Redfield Reform Recommendation

#*9* *Every noncandidate group or entity that gives more than $3,000 to candidates or political committees during a six-month period should be required to form a political committee and file reports of receipts and expenditures as specified by the State Election Code.*

Under current law, candidates who raise or spend more that $3,000 in a 12-month reporting period are required to form political committees and disclose their receipts and expenditures through periodic reports. The requirements for noncandidate committees are less certain. Most groups and associations form committees under the state law and file reports. Some unions and corporations form committees and file reports. But most do not. Some labor unions do not file reports under an interpretation of the law by the State Board of Elections that holds that if the sources of contributions come only from members of the union, and if the union's contributions are reported by the candidates who receive them, then it is not necessary for the unions to file reports. Using the same logic, some corporations make individual contributions to associations that make lump-sum contributions to political committees that contribute to candidates. The names of the individual corporations are not reported in these situations. It is critical to any system of reporting and disclosure that the sources of contributions are clear and unambiguous. Having all contributors file also allows for cross-checking between what candidates say they received and what contributors say they gave. This makes the system more accurate. This proposed rule should not apply to individuals acting on their own behalf, but it should apply to individual corporations and unions as well as to groups and associations.

RRR

Redfield Reform Recommendation

#10 *The official name of any noncandidate committee must reflect the source of the funding for the committee, and contributions made by a noncandidate committee must be made and reported using the official name. Also, the purpose given in the organizational documents filed by the committee with the State Board of Elections when forming a political committee must reflect the specific interests of the contributors.*

Under the current system, it is possible to hide the true source of funds by funneling them through a committee with an ambiguous name (The Motherhood and Apple Pie PAC), even if the committee is organized under the State Election Code and files reports with the State Board of Elections. Political committees formed under current law do not have to reflect the source of their contributions in their names unless a single source makes up more than one-third of the total receipts. The purpose listed in the organization document can be very general. For example, under year 2001 laws and practices, payday and title loan companies can form a political committee, call it the ISLA PAC, list the purpose of the committee as supporting candidates and issues consistent with the goals of the ISLA, and give contributions under the name ISLA without identifying in their organization documents or by their name the interests of their major contributors and the specific purpose of the group. A commitment to full disclosure demands that anyone seeing an ISLA contribution or examining the group's reports through the State Board of Elections' web site would know that ISLA stands for the Illinois Small Loan Association and that the political committee was formed to promote the interests of payday and title loan companies.

Redfield Reform Recommendation

11 *If a candidate or party committee does not have address or occupation and employer information for any individual giving an itemized contribution of more than $500, then those committees should not be allowed to spend the money until they obtain the information.*

Campaigns are now required to report on their pre-election and semi-annual reports the addresses for the sources of all itemized contributions and the occupation and employer of every individual who contributes more than $500. Repeated failure to make a good-faith effort to find out this information and include it in their pre-election and semi-annual reports may trigger fines from the State Board of Elections. A better enforcement approach would be to require that money be held in escrow until the information is obtained.

It is also the case that occupation and employer information that is required for contributions over $500 in pre-election and semi-annual reports is not required when those contributions are reported just prior to an election. Pre-election campaign reports are due to the Board of Elections 15 days before an election, and must reflect the campaign finance status at 30 days prior to the election. But, campaigns are also currently required to report all contributions over $500 received in the 30 days prior to the election. These contributions must be reported within two business days through a report called an A-1. But contributions disclosed on the A-1 reports are exempt from the occupation and employer disclosure requirement that applies to pre-election and semi-annual reports. A requirement that a "good-faith effort" be made within the two-day reporting period to provide occupation and employer information for contributions over $500 as reported on the A-1 form would help give a more complete pre-election picture of who a candidate's contributors are. However, such a requirement should not prohibit the spending of the money or be used to delay the reporting of the contribution.

Recommendations for More Timely Disclosure

We need to make disclosed information more complete. Most important, though, we need to make reporting more timely. This criticism applies not only to campaign contributions and expenditures, but to records of the roll-call votes made by state legislators. At the local level, rules for timely vote disclosure can extend to county boards and city councils. Timely information should be readily available in electronic form. The following changes would increase the flow of information to voters and enhance the quality of their participation in the process. The changes would also strengthen self-regulation and enhance overall citizen confidence in the political process.

┌───┐
│   **RRR**   │
│   │
│   **Redfield Reform Recommendation**   │
│ **#12** *Adopt a transaction-based reporting system that requires all political committees that are required to file electronically to report all transactions (receipts and expenditures) within 30 days of their occurrence. Retain the current requirement that aggregate contributions (including in-kind and loans) of $500 or more received within 30 days preceding an election must be reported within two business days and posted immediately by the State Board of Elections.* │
└───┘

As of the year 2001, the law requires comprehensive reports of receipts and expenditures by candidate and noncandidate committees to be filed 30 days after each six-month reporting period. Pre-election reports of receipts and transfers of funds that cover the period from the beginning of the reporting period up to four weeks before a primary or general election are required 15 days prior to a primary or general election. Contributions of $500 or more received after the pre-election reporting period must be reported within two working days. There is less information about contributions made during the spring and fall legislative sessions. The electronic filing of pre-election reports in the spring and fall of even-numbered years does provide some picture of who contributed how much money between January and the first of March and between July and the first of October. But in odd-numbered (non-election) years, no interim reports are required during the spring or fall legislative sessions. So, right now, the best information about who is funding elections is therefore available after primary and general elections take place, not before. Just as troubling, information about who is making contributions when the legislature is in session is largely unavailable until months after the legislature leaves Springfield.

Adopting a transaction-based reporting system will help get information out while elections are still being contested and issues are still in play. For example, a contribution from a tobacco manufacturer to a party leader made in the second week of February would become a matter of public record by the third week of March, while any tobacco-friendly legislation was still being considered in the state legislature. People could then decide for themselves — as this issue was happening — whether there might be a connection between the tobacco contribution and the fate of the tobacco-related legislation. This, then, is the advantage of adopting a system of rolling reports. Citizens would have a clear opportunity to draw their own conclusions between current policy measures and campaign contributions. They would also have a more complete picture of who is funding political campaigns.

Finally, as a practical matter, I would suggest that under this proposal all transactions (except contributions of $500 or more received within 30 days of an election) reported to the State Board of Elections be held for seven days and then posted on the board's web site. The seven-day hold would allow the campaign committee time to ensure the accuracy of the report before it is posted.

RRR

Redfield Reform Recommendation

 # _13_ *Require political committees for candidates who have filed for elective office to report all transactions electronically within 14 days of receipt during the 60 days prior to the date of the primary election and the 60 days prior to the date of the general election. All transactions (except the receipt of contributions of $500 or more) that take place within 14 days of a primary or general election would not have to be reported until 14 days after the election.*

As the time of elections draws nearer, the state should adopt a shorter transaction schedule for candidates. This would provide a rolling report that would reveal a moving picture of late-campaign contributions and spending. In the year 2001, citizens have, at best, a snapshot picture, which they receive every three to six months, depending on the schedule of elections.

RRR

Redfield Reform Recommendation

#14 *Require that roll call votes of the Illinois General Assembly be posted on the Internet within 24 hours of the vote. Require that a cumulative database of roll-call votes be available to the general public in a standard electronic format on a weekly basis.*

While roll call votes are a matter of public record, getting access to them in a timely manner and in a useable form is difficult at best. While the voting in the General Assembly is by electronic roll call, as of the year 2001 the records for the Senate votes are available only in hard copy. House records are slightly better. They were posted on the Internet, beginning in April of 2000. However, they are in text form, rather than in a searchable database. Making this information available in a timely manner on the Internet and in a searchable database that can be purchased by groups and individuals would allow everyone to explore the linkages between campaign contributions and public policy.

The Road to Reform

Working on the margins of an issue is a time-consuming, often frustrating process. But with a strategy and a focus, change can beget change. Prior to 1997, Illinois law required citizens to provide personal information before they were allowed to examine campaign finance reports. Each person had to fill out a Form D-3 that asked for his or her name, address, phone number, and occupation, as well as the name of his or her employer. Citizens also had to list the reason that they wanted to see the campaign finance report. Then, a copy of the D-3 would be forwarded to the committees whose records the citizen examined — all this at a time when contributors to political campaigns were not required to list their occupations or employers.

The very fact that the state required citizens to file D-3s is a perfect reflection of a politics that is designed for the insiders (the professionals) and a politics that actively discourages citizen (amateur) involvement. But, in isolation, such a requirement became impossible to defend. When public interest groups and the news media drew widespread public attention to the D-3 requirements, eliminating that form became part of the 1997 campaign finance reform measure that was signed into law. The abolition of the D-3 was also included in the measure because it seemed like such a minor thing to give up. The same reform bill that killed the D-3 required the State Board of Elections to put campaign finance information on the Internet, but it did not provide any changes in the filing process. In essence, that reform measure was, on its surface, mild enough to get legislative support. Undoubtedly, some of those who grudgingly supported the 1997 changes clearly hoped that afterwards the issue would go away, since the legislature had passed "campaign finance reform." After all, passing a largely symbolic bill to placate an agitated public is an old legislative maneuver.

But the seemingly benign elimination of the D-3 has had a cumulative effect. Its abolition removed a legal barrier that would have made it very difficult for the public to have access to the database of campaign receipts being developed by staff of the State Board of Elections. Once State Board of Elections staff constructed the database and made it available to the public, there was a quantum increase in information about campaign contributions, which public interest groups, public officials, and the press used to promote further changes in the campaign finance system. The door was open for electronic filing proposals and the appetite of the press and public interest groups was whetted for more information. No one holding public office could go on record as opposing more complete and timely disclosure. The results were more changes in 1998, including construction of a system for mandatory electronic filing and the creation of an Internet web site that gives the public access to that filing information. Illinois' system of electronic filing is the envy of most states and the federal system.

The public access and attention generated by these changes have moved the role of money in politics from the periphery to the center of political discussion in Illinois. The modest proposals suggested in the previous pages of this chapter look doable in the evolving political climate. Five years ago, they would have seemed radical and impossible. Sometimes a strategy of picking off the weak links is more productive than a frontal assault.

Ultimately, campaign finance reform is both a vision and a process. It is a vision because there are a number of ways to achieve the broad goals of encouraging participation in the political process and building and then maintaining the support of citizens for the political process. The vision extends across the country, though the goals might best be achieved through different means in different states or at the national level. Because campaign finance reform deals with fundamental and often conflicting values — participation, access, competition, free speech, property rights — all proposals and systems are subject to legitimate questions as to why one principle or goal is preferred over another. If ever there were a policy area where the perfect is the enemy of the good, it is campaign finance reform. Change requires choices among several worthy values.

Campaign finance reform is a process because, given the constitutional framework set by the U.S. Supreme Court, it will always be possible for those with money to play whatever system is in place. With enough resources and determination, they will be able to beat the system — not in the sense of always winning, but in terms of maximizing the advantage that those with money have over those without money. What works to achieve the broad goals of campaign finance reform in Illinois this year or this decade may not work in the same way as the political process evolves. Illinois reforms may not work at all in other states or at the federal level. Those in Illinois who seek reform have to be prepared to monitor changes and revisit and remake the system on a regular basis.

It would be nice to say that a single proposal would magically remake the Illinois political system, and it would be especially nice to say that proposal will appear next year. It won't. But change *will* come. Five years ago I was filling out hundreds of D-3 forms every six months just to gain the right to look at campaign finance reports that chronicled outrageous personal-use spending by legislators. Back then, everyone told me that the system would never change because, "This is Illinois." Today, we have electronic filing, a new ethics law, an ever-growing public debate over the role of money in Illinois politics, and the legislature now — at least sometimes — seriously considers finance reform proposals. Yes, this is still Illinois. But Illinois always will be exactly what we make of her.

Works Cited

Before listing the sources for each chapter, a note about the figures used in this book is in order. All dollar figures, unless otherwise noted, were generated from an Illinois campaign finance database created by the author. Support for the database was provided by The Joyce Foundation and the Institute for Public Affairs at the University of Illinois at Springfield. The database contains receipt and expenditure records beginning with January 1, 1993, and is updated every six months. As of August 2000, the database contained more than 400,000 records from more than 600 candidates for legislative and statewide offices.

CHAPTER 1

Elazar, Daniel J. 1996. Series introduction for *Illinois Politics and Government: The Expanding Metropolitan Frontier,* by Samuel K. Gove and James D. Nowlan. Lincoln, NB and London: University of Nebraska Press.

Fenton, John H. 1966. *Midwest Politics.* New York: Holt, Rinehart and Winston.

Gove, Samuel K., and James D. Nowlan. 1996. *Illinois Politics and Government: The Expanding Metropolitan Frontier.* Lincoln, NB and London: University of Nebraska Press.

Hartley, Robert E. 1999. *Paul Powell of Illinois: A Lifelong Democrat.* Carbondale and Edwardsville, IL: Southern Illinois University Press.

Howard, Robert P. 1999. *Mostly Good and Competent Men,* second edition. Springfield, IL: The Institute for Public Affairs, University of Illinois at Springfield.

Illinois Issues. 2000. Scandal by Number. May, 38.

Merriner, James L. 1999. *Mr. Chairman: Power in Dan Rostenkowski's America.* Carbondale and Edwardsville, IL: Southern Illinois University Press.

Simpson, Burney. 1999a. Gambling. *Illinois Issues,* June, 10.

Simpson, Burney. 1999b. Liquor & soft drinks. *Illinois Issues,* June, 10.

CHAPTER 2

Alexander, Herbert E. 1991. *Reform and Reality: The Financing of State and Local Campaigns*. St. Fredrick, MD: Twentieth Century Fund Press.

Dreyfuss, Robert. 1999. Reform Gets Rolling: Campaign Finance at the Grass Roots. *The American Prospect* 54, July-August.

Federal Election Commission Advisory Opinion. 1975. *Federal Register* 45292 vol. 23, Sun PAC, 40.

Fitzgerald, Jay. 1994. Fundraisers: Just Part of the Game. *The State Journal-Register*, Springfield, IL, May 22, 7.

Gurwitt, Rob. 1992. The Mirage of Campaign Reform. *Governing*, August, 48-55.

Malbin, Michael J., and Thomas L. Gais. 1998. *The Day After Reform: Sobering Campaign Finance Lessons for the American States*. Albany, NY: Rockefeller Institute Press.

Sorauf, Frank J. 1988. *Money in American Elections*. Glenview, IL: Scott Foresman and Co.

CHAPTER 5

Ekert, Toby. 1997. Unplugging the Electric Power Monopolies. *Illinois Issues*. January, 12-15.

Finke, Doug. 2000. MSI Co-Conspirators Named. *State Journal-Register*. August 24.

Freedman, Anne. 1994. *Patronage: An American Tradition*. Chicago: Nelson-Hall Publishers.

Gibson, Ray. 1999. Driver Admits Ignoring Warning Before Crash. *Chicago Tribune*. October 5.

Grumman, Cornelia, and Melita Maria Garza. 1999. License-Selling Scandal Figure Going to Prison. *Chicago Tribune*. February 27.

Hammett, Jim. 2000. Illinois Judge Grants Injunction in K-J Lawsuit. *Wine Today* (digital edition at WineToday.com). January 4.

Works Cited

Illinois Issues. 1997. Lawmakers Deregulate Electric Utilities, Tighten Rules on State Contracts and Hog Farms. December, 11.

Illinois Issues. 2000. Scandal by Number. March, 42.

Illinois Issues. 2000. Scandal by the Number. April, 43.

Illinois Issues. 2000. Scandal by the Number. September, 36.

Keith, Ryan. 2000. State May Muzzle Payday Lenders. *State Journal-Register.* August 28, 1, 4.

Long, Ray. 1998. MSI Corruption Probe Concludes. *Chicago Tribune.* December 22.

Long, Ray. 2000. MSI Scandal Link to Aides of Edgar, Philip Revealed. *Chicago Tribune.* August 24.

Long, Ray, and Christi Parsons. 2000. Ryan: Corruption Part of License Office Culture. *Chicago Tribune.* March 8.

Man, Anthony. 1997. Can the Utilities Strike a Deal with Lawmakers? *Illinois Issues.* October, 24-26.

O'Connor, Matt. 1999. Witness Links Trucker to Bribe. *Chicago Tribune.* September 27.

Pearson, Rick. 1997. Cable's Capitol Reception. *Chicago Tribune.* November 9.

Pearson, Rick, and Christi Parsons. 1997. MSI Verdicts Jolt Springfield. *Chicago Tribune.* August 17.

United States Attorney, Northern District of Illinois. 1999. Operation Safe Road Summary. Personal communication. December 14.

CHAPTER 6

Everson, David. 1996. COOGA Redux? In *Almanac of Illinois Politics — 1996,* by Craig A. Roberts and Paul Kleppner. Springfield, IL: The Institute for Public Affairs, University of Illinois at Springfield.

Pensoneau, Taylor. 1997. *Governor Richard Ogilvie: In the Interest of the State.* Carbondale and Edwardsville, IL: Southern Illinois University Press.

Redfield, Kent. 1998. What Keeps the Four Tops on Top?
Leadership and Power in the Illinois General Assembly. In
Almanac of Illinois Politics — 1998, by David A. Joens and
Paul Kleppner. Springfield, IL: The Institute for Public
Affairs, University of Illinois at Springfield.

Wheeler, Charles N., III. 1982. Redistricting '81: A Democratic
Decade? In *Illinois Elections*, edited by Caroline A.
Gherardini, J. Michael Lennon, Richard J. Shereikis, and
Larry R. Smith. Springfield, IL: *Illinois Issues* magazine,
Sangamon State University.

Index

A

B

C

189

Index

Illinois Manufacturers' Association (IMA), 49, 51, 52, 58, 64, 65, 100, 105, 133, 143

Illinois New Car and Truck Dealers Association, 60, 117-120

Illinois Power, 31, 51, 62, 131-133, 136

Illinois Racing Association, 142

Illinois Retail Merchants Association, 54

Illinois Small Loan Association (ISLA), 135, 136, 137, 168, 176

Illinois State Bar Association, 31

Illinois State Gaming Board, 148

Illinois State Lottery, 139

Illinois State Medical Society, 49, 51, 52, 57, 58, 65, 98, 100, 105, 143

Illinois State Supreme Court, 29, 106, 107, 108, 111, 114, 166, 171

Illinois Trial Lawyers Association, 51, 52, 58, 65, 98, 100, 101

Illinova Corporation, 51, 131

IMA, *see* Illinois Manufacturers' Association

incumbency,
    challenges to, 80, 82, 86, 94, 173
    re-election advantage of, 79, 81, 89-90, 97, 113

independent expenditures, 27, 74

Independent Voters of Illinois - Independent Precinct Organizations (IVI - IPO), 13

individualistic political culture, 9-12

in-kind contributions or services, 33, 35, 56

inseverability clause, 147

Institute for Public Affairs, 47, 77, 117

IRMA, *see* Illinois Retail Merchants Association

ISLA, *see* Illinois Small Loan Association

issue ads, 23, 27, 170

itemized contributions, 35, 47

itemized expenditures, 35

IVI - IPO, *see* Independent Voters of Illinois - Independent Precinct Organizations

IWAPAC, 127, 129

J

Joliet, Illinois, 141, 150

Jones, Emil, 91, 121, 124, 127, 128, 129, 132, 141

Jones, John, 91

Joyce Foundation, The, 47, 77, 117

Judge & Dolph, Ltd., 126, 127, 130

judicial elections, 77, 106-113, 114, 166, 170-172

K

Kendall-Jackson Wine Estates, 130

Kentucky Derby, 148

Kerner, Otto, 4, 5

Klingler, Gwenn, 89

Kurtz, Rosemary, 98

L

labor unions, *see* unions

Ladd, Bill, 151, 152

Lake County, 142

193

Index

Republican National Committee, 73
retention elections, 108
Righter, Dale, 92, 93
riverboat casinos, 6, 61, 137-149, 150
Rock, Philip, 128
Rockford, Illinois, 54
roll call votes, 43, 177, 180
Ronan, Al, 38
Rosemont, Illinois, 139, 146, 147, 148
Rostenkowski, Dan, 4, 82
RPAC, *see* Illinois Association of Realtors
Rutan v. The Republican Party of Illinois, 8, 11
Ryan, George, 4, 5, 7, 38, 47, 54, 67, 73, 77, 104, 105, 117, 124, 125, 127, 129, 139, 140, 150, 154, 155, 160
Ryan Holding Company of Illinois, 102
Ryan, Jim, 123

S

safe districts, 87, *see also* legislative redistricting
Sandburg, Carl, 11
Santos, Miriam, 104
scandals, 14, 15, 120, 149-155
Schedule A, 33
Schedule A-1, 32, 33, 34
Schedule B, 33
Schedule C, 33, 35
Schedule I, 33, 35
Schmidt, John, 104
school finance reform, 160
school vouchers, 160

Securities and Exchange Commission, 149
semi-annual campaign finance reports, 33, 34, *see also* D-2 form
Service Employees International Union Illinois Council, 102
severability clause, 147
Simon, Paul, 3, 13, 40
single-issue groups, 49, 64
single-member districts, 160
Skinner, Cal, Jr., 98
Skokie, Illinois, 42
soft money, 24, 27, 74
Sommer, Keith, 96
Soto, Cynthia, 98
spending limits, 22, 25, 27, 163, 170
Sportsman's Park, 142
Springfield, Illinois, 59, 88, 93, 95, 117, 118, 126, 128, 136, 152, 153
State Board of Elections, 5, 28, 29, 30, 31, 32, 33, 40, 41, 42, 135, 175, 176, 178, 179, 181
state budget, 7
State Election Code, 174, 176
Stephens, Donald, 142, 147
Stevenson, Adlai, 3
stick system of campaign finance regulation, 25, 36
stranded costs, 133
Stride, Christopher, 96
Sun Oil Company, 24
sunshine system of campaign finance regulation, 24-25, 26, 36
Supreme Court, *see* Illinois State Supreme Court *or* United States Supreme Court

T

targeted legislative races, 5, 13, 63, 70, 72, 86, 90-95, 114

Teamsters Drive Political Fund, 102

Texas, 36, 126

Thomas, Bob, 110

Thompson, Jim, 11, 66, 84, 128, 129, 160

Thrall Car Manufacturing, 143, 144

TIP, *see* Hotel Employees and Restaurant Employees International Union Tip Education Fund

transaction-based reporting system, 178

transfers of campaign funds, 19, 27, 33, 35, 68-73, 91

U

Unicom, 51, 131

unions, 26, 27, 31, 47, 49, 50, 56, 63, 67, 101, 102, 163, 169, 170, 175

United Auto Workers Illinois PAC, 102

United Food and Commercial Workers Local 881, 102

United Parcel Service, 102

United States Constitution, *see* Constitution of the United States

United States Postal Service, 72

United States Supreme Court, 8, 11, 20, 21, 22, 23, 26, 170, 182

University of Illinois, 147

University of Illinois at Springfield, 47, 77, 117

V

Vermont, 27

Vienna, Illinois, 3

voter participation, 163, 164, 167, 170, 182

voters guides, 173-174

W

Walker, Daniel, 29, 83, 84, 103

Walker v. State Board of Elections, 29, 40

Watergate scandal, 19, 20

Welfare reform, 10

Wheaton, Bonnie, 110

White, Jesse, 67, 68

Willis, Duane, 153

Willis, Janet, 153

Wine and Spirits Distributors of Illinois (WSDI), 127

Wine and Spirits Industry Fair Dealing Act (Wirtz bill), 6, 125-131, 156

Winston and Strawn, 128

Wirtz bill, *see* Wine and Spirits Industry Fair Dealing Act

Wirtz Corporation, 126-130

Wirtz, William, 6, 126, 128, 130

Wisconsin, 126

Woodward, Pam, 93

WSDI, *see* Wine and Spirits Distributors of Illinois

Z

Zwick, Morton, 110

ABOUT THE INSTITUTE FOR PUBLIC AFFAIRS

Because of its location in the state capital, the University of Illinois at Springfield has a special mission in public affairs. To fulfill its mission, the campus directs educational, research, and service efforts to help solve problems facing the state and nearby communities. The Institute for Public Affairs is a primary vehicle through which the campus carries out these public affairs activities.

The Institute for Public Affairs houses the Springfield campus's major public affairs units: the Center for Legal Studies, the Graduate Intern Programs, *Illinois Issues*, the Illinois Legislative Studies Center, the Office of Policy and Administrative Studies, the Survey Research Office, the Television Office, and radio stations WUIS/WIPA. These units are coordinated by the Institute's Central Office.

In cooperation with the Institute for Public Affairs' Editorial Board, the Institute also oversees the publication and dissemination of works designed to enhance citizen awareness of issues, policy, and the history of Illinois government.

For more information, go to the institute's publications web site at www.ipapublications.uis.edu.

About the Author

Kent Redfield is a professor of
Political Studies at the University of Illinois
at Springfield (UIS), where he is also the
associate director of the Illinois Legislative
Studies Center. He received his undergradu-
ate degree in political science from the
University of Utah and his M.A. and Ph.D.
in political science from the University of
Washington. Prior to joining the UIS faculty
in 1979, he worked for four years as a mem-
ber of the research/appropriations staff for the speaker of the
Illinois General Assembly.

Redfield co-wrote *Lawmaking in Illinois,* and he contributes to
the biennial *Almanac of Illinois Politics,* which is now in its sixth edition. He has been researching campaign finance in Illinois since
1991. His findings have been presented in numerous research
reports, a series of articles in *Illinois Issues* magazine, and *Cash
Clout,* a 1994 book on financing legislative elections in Illinois.

In 1995 and 1996, he served as the research director for the
Illinois Campaign Finance Task Force. This project examined the
role of money in Illinois politics and was funded by The Joyce
Foundation. The task force, which was chaired by former U.S.
Senator Paul Simon and former Illinois Governor William Stratton,
issued its recommendations in early 1997 in a report titled *Tainted
Democracy.*

In the fall of 1997, Redfield received a grant from The Joyce
Foundation to fund the Sunshine Project to increase public aware-
ness and knowledge of the role of money in Illinois politics.
Funding for the project was recently renewed through 2001.